YOU

are not

FORGOTTEN

YOU

are not

FORGOTTEN

DISCOVERING
THE GOD WHO SEES
THE OVERLOOKED
AND DISREGARDED

CHRISTINE HOOVER

B&H
PUBLISHING
BRENTWOOD, TENNESSEE

Published by B&H Publishing Group
Brentwood, Tennessee

Dewey Decimal Classification: 155.9
Subject Heading: LONELINESS / SOLITUDE / ASSURANCE
(THEOLOGY)

Cover design and illustration by Geraldine Sy/Good Illustration.
Author photo by NAMB staff.

1 2 3 4 5 6 7 • 27 26 25 24

To the God who has made it clear he sees me

I will rejoice and be glad in your faithful love
because you have seen my affliction.
You know the troubles of my soul
and have not handed me over to the enemy.
You have set my feet in a spacious place.

PSALM 31:7–8

CONTENTS

Part Five: Restored Vision

Part One

OVERLOOKED, DISREGARDED, AND HURTING

Chapter 1

LOST AND LANGUISHING
IN UNSEENNESS

I awoke in a panic, my heart racing and a deep twinge wringing my insides. Still hovering in the liminal space between sleep and full consciousness, anguish flooded over me as my mind caught up to my body, and I began recalling the details of the dream from which I'd just awoken.

In the dream, I'd been at a church gathering with my husband, surrounded by people who were scurrying around, happily purposeful in their activity and conversation, a merry band of brothers and sisters—people I knew and loved in my real life. I, however, stood apart and alone. As an outside observer of myself in the dream, I could feel the deep sadness and aching need emanating from my solitary place. A growing, sinister vine encircled my feet, threatening to entangle me and pull me under until I disappeared altogether.

Certainly, someone around me could feel the pulsating sadness, for I seemed to be the black cloud in their sunshine.

Certainly, someone would notice I was slowly disappearing, my voice increasingly muted. But no one saw or spoke to me.

I began to plead for help, for someone to see, and I turned in expectation to my husband, Kyle. He did not have time, he said, gesturing at the people dependent on him. I persisted, my volume growing to a shriek, but he became increasingly mute and stone-faced, unwilling to hear, refusing to continue the conversation, eager to attend elsewhere. I acknowledged that he *did* have so much to do—he was, as their pastor, managing the people and their activity around us. Perhaps I'd become a burden—a hindrance to his important work, even to his calling. Perhaps I was asking for too much. Perhaps I was being selfish or too emotional. So I quieted myself, trying not to need.

But the sadness, oh the sadness, of being left to fend for myself! The sadness grew so palpable that it had grabbed my hand and yanked me out of my dream and into the shadows of the early morning.

My husband slept peacefully beside me, unaware of the unkind person he'd been to me in my dream, and as I listened for his breathing in the dark, I remembered it was not real and began coaxing my anger, loneliness, and sadness to return to their hiding places.

Soon after, the alarm went off, and as we traipsed to the coffeepot together, I said with a knowing smile, "I had the dream again." It had become a joke between us that I only ever have bad dreams and that he was the recurring villain in them.

In truth, I had the same dream: the details were always slightly different, but in each one I was alone in a group of people, shrieking for someone to see me, listen to me, or help me. Within the group of people were always specific friends or family members I turned to for help who, annoyed by my need, acted as if I were invisible.

Each time I awoke from this recurring dream, I told myself what we all tell ourselves when we have vivid nightmares: *it's not real. You're safe. Nothing about this is true.*

And I believed that for good reasons.

Because when I awoke in that bed and in that house, I awoke to a happy marriage of over two decades, three incredible sons, and a pinch-me kind of writing and speaking career. My husband and I had planted a church together that was, by all accounts, thriving and healthy. I'd been raised in a loving Christian family, and I had a stable of women beside and supportively behind me that I considered deep, lifelong friends. In no way could someone like me legitimately feel unseen and sad. I'd been blessed beyond measure, so what was all this nightmare shrieking about?

Sadness Tried to Speak

I discovered what the shrieking was about in a painful way, one that drove me to a counselor's couch.

The counselor, after spending time with me, listening to my story, and asking a few clarifying questions, sat quietly for a moment before asking the most salient question of all: "Christine, what is your deepest wound?"

I hesitated. In characteristic fashion, I was searching frantically for the correct answer.

"I don't know," I said, unable to find it.

"It is, of course, that you've not been seen."

He was the type of counselor I'd trusted immediately—gentle, insightful, careful to gather details before dispensing words. In other words, a good one. So when he said so matter-of-factly that I'd legitimately gone unseen, I felt a dart land in the small red circle in the dead center of the dart board of my heart, and I immediately began weeping.

My mind ran through the events of the previous years, and I recalled the occasional revealing thoughts I'd expressed to Kyle and to friends in vulnerable moments. I recognized that my sadness had been trying to tell me about itself for a while. I'd refused to validate my own feelings and experiences. Instead, I'd believed others when they'd said I was too much and not enough and too emotional. I'd believed they were right when they said it's not a big deal and I should get over it. I'd believed them when they said that what I wanted or thought or felt wasn't valid. I'd believed them when they said I had value but should endlessly wait my turn. I'd believed them that I was selfish and should go on dying to myself until I was but a shadow.

So I'd become a shadow.

There was a reason, in other words, for my sadness.

"Yes, and I think there is a value component to not being seen," I said in response to the counselor, considering the exact shading of my sadness.

"Yes," he said. "It's a refusing to see. Others have refused to see you when you've asked them to see."

He was right. I'd been severely wounded by important people in my life refusing to see me. When I'd given them opportunity to see and sometimes even begged them to see, they'd turned away, just like in my dream. They'd deflected, blamed, or made it about them. As a result, I'd felt invalidated, confused, and unworthy of love.

In response, I'd contorted myself into uncomfortable shapes, attempting to be seen in ways acceptable to those important people, and I hid away the (good and right) parts of me they'd invalidated. I'd become an expert at it, so much so that I couldn't even *see myself* any longer.

In other words, I'd not only become a shadow; I'd also learned to hide in the shadows. I'd *allowed* myself to go unseen by others because it was too risky to do otherwise—when I fought to be heard, the pain of apathy or invalidation awaited me.

However, I'd not only contorted myself but also distorted myself; in order to be seen and valued, I'd taken up sinful overreactions that had compounded my own pain.

Seeing it all so clearly for the first time there on the counselor's couch, I could not contain the tears.

The Woman Who Named God

I finally let the wound gape open, only because every stitch I'd doctored myself with over the years burst apart, and every salve I'd applied I could see had been meaningless self-soothing.

And as I did, a God-whisper filled my mind: *I see.* The air between us became charged, as if he had waited for the moment the air finally hit the uncovered wound. The wound, as wounds do, pulsed with pain, each beat of my heart remembering specific ways I had been unseen and finally allowing myself to name those ways as legitimate wounds. On the upbeat, however, there was a response that became a refrain of hope: *I saw. And I see.*

I see. This was not wishful thinking. God was whispering his own written Word into my ear.

When a biblical reference comes to mind, I know the Holy Spirit has come to my side with an invitation. Sometimes it's an invitation to repentance; other times it's an invitation to receive comfort from God. This, I knew, was an invitation to both a bedrock truth and a healing comfort, so the moment I returned home from the counselor's couch, I tore through my Bible to Genesis 16:13 (NIV): "[Hagar] gave this name to the LORD who spoke to her: 'You are the God who sees me,' for she said, 'I have now seen the One who sees me.'"

The God Who Sees. That is his name.

The God Who Sees me. That's what he does.

I'd read this story in Genesis many times, but perhaps stopped for the first time to intently observe Hagar. Who was this woman who spoke these words and knew with such assurance that she was seen by God? How did she feel so confident in her "seenness" that she presumed to give God a nickname, and a personal one at that?

We might imagine she had such confidence to name God because she was a queen or princess, a daughter of noble birth, or some other visibly important woman, but Hagar was a simple servant girl, an Egyptian stranger in a strange land, and a person of low rank who lacked influence, power, money, and social standing. We're only introduced to her because she lived with Abram and Sarai (later Abraham and Sarah, the father and mother of the Jewish race):

> Abram's wife, Sarai, had not borne any children for him, but she owned an Egyptian slave named Hagar. Sarai said to Abram, "Since the LORD has

prevented me from bearing children, go to my
slave; perhaps through her I can build a family."
And Abram agreed to what Sarai said. So Abram's
wife, Sarai, took Hagar, her Egyptian slave, and
gave her to her husband, Abram, as a wife for
him. This happened after Abram had lived in the
land of Canaan ten years. He slept with Hagar,
and she became pregnant. When she saw that she
was pregnant, her mistress became contemptible to her. Then Sarai said to Abram, "You are
responsible for my suffering! I put my slave in
your arms, and when she saw that she was pregnant, I became contemptible to her. May the
LORD judge between me and you.'
    Abram replied to Sarai, "Here, your slave is
in your power; do whatever you want with her."
Then Sarai mistreated her so much that she ran
away from her. (Gen. 16:1–6)

Prior to Hagar's entrance into the biblical narrative, God
had promised Abram a son. From this son, God said, Abram's
offspring would become as numerous as the stars in the sky.
Although Abram and Sarai were childless and far past childbear-
ing age, Abram believed God could and would fulfill his promise,
and God was pleased with Abram's faith.[1]

By the time Hagar entered the narrative, the promise of a
child was ten years old, ten years unfulfilled. A decade would've
been a frightening alarm bell for Sarai because in ancient Near

---

1. Genesis 15:4–6.

Eastern culture, if a wife was barren, the husband could marry a second wife and, after a ten-year period of barrenness, he could divorce her.[2] So, in her distress, Sarai seized upon another culturally acceptable custom: she gave her servant girl to Abram as a concubine in order to produce the promised child.

Hagar's subsequent pregnancy and Sarai's choice introduced chaos into her family life. One sinful choice became the first domino of many to fall. Sarai sinned by taking matters away from God and into her own hands, blaming Abram when her plan backfired, and treating Hagar harshly when she felt threatened at losing her rightful place in the family. Abram sinned by passively following Sarai's lead and then refusing responsibility for the well-being of Hagar and his child when Sarai became angry. Hagar sinned by cursing Sarai in contempt, a sin God could not and would not overlook.[3]

Hagar, however, was in an especially desperate situation because Abram's child growing in her womb, by custom, belonged to Abram's wife, Sarai.[4] What would become of her when the child was born? Abram had given Sarai permission to do whatever she pleased with Hagar, and she'd already proven her intent. Who would see Hagar in her lowly state and in her desperate situation and provide for her? Who would advocate for her and her unborn child? No one, and she knew it as sure as the sun would rise the next morning.

2. Kenneth A. Mathews, *Genesis 11:27–50:26*, vol. 1b, The New American Commentary Series (Nashville: B&H, 2005), 184–85.

3. Genesis 12:1–3.

4. R. C. Sproul et al, eds., *The Reformation Study Bible* (Nashville: Thomas Nelson, 1995). As found on biblegateway.com.

So she fled, alone and pregnant, attempting to make her way through the desert back to her home country. No one went after her to make sure she remained alive. No one considered how she might feel. No one tried to talk her into returning home. No one treated her as an existent human being, much less a vulnerable woman carrying a baby.

She was completely hopeless and all alone.

An unseen person.

Seen and Sent Back

Have you ever been in a situation like Hagar's? Perhaps you fled from a painful relationship, or you felt shoved out into a type of wilderness by the sinful choices of another. Perhaps your own contempt of God and his ways sent you on a long, winding journey away from home and into the unrelenting heat of the desert.

All of us in some way experience desert times; it's the human condition to encounter bumps and bruises in life. But sometimes there is a unique weight to our suffering, and the understanding that we alone must carry it can easily create a sense of being hidden and vulnerable: being a single mom in a sea of married couples on Sunday morning, caring for an elderly parent or small children around the clock, living with chronic pain, raising a child with special needs, being sidelined in the workplace, marking off another year of childlessness, standing in the spotlight but being unknown, or being an older woman in a culture that values youth.

The list could go on indefinitely.

Though we all live with unique circumstances that make us feel different or "other," unseenness is something more. Unseenness occurs when an important part of who we are or what we've experienced is misunderstood, unacknowledged, unappreciated, unprotected, invalidated, or uncultivated by important people in our lives. As I told my counselor, unseenness has a value component: the message we receive is that we aren't worthy to be heard or cared for and that our needs and feelings aren't valid.

If you have picked up this book, I imagine you've done so because you're hurting. You may never have developed a definition of unseenness, but I imagine you've felt the pain of it and have managed your life around those feelings. I want to say that I'm sorry you've walked through or are walking through unseenness. The pain of feeling unseen is one of the deepest pains because not only are your circumstances difficult but your feelings about them are often misunderstood or unacknowledged, leading to silence and shadows. There are things you cannot say. There is the feeling of hot shame that fills your body when you remember, the constant fight to forgive and, sometimes, just to show up. There is the feeling of being marked and labeled, the longing for a kind word or to be who you used to be back when you were full of life and vitality.

When we find ourselves in the desert of unseenness, everything seems dry and colorless. Hopeless. Sad.

But, friend, you are alive. Look at what you've survived. You are here.

And someone else is, too.

> The angel of the LORD found [Hagar] by a spring
> in the wilderness, the spring on the way to Shur.
> He said, "Hagar, slave of Sarai, where have you
> come from and where are you going?"

She replied, "I'm running away from my mistress Sarai."

The angel of the LORD said to her, "Go back to your mistress and submit to her authority." The angel of the LORD said to her, "I will greatly multiply your offspring, and they will be too many to count."

The angel of the LORD said to her, "You have conceived and will have a son. You will name him Ishmael [God Hears], for the LORD has heard your cry of affliction. This man will be like a wild donkey. His hand will be against everyone, and everyone's hand will be against him; he will settle near all his relatives."

So she named the LORD who spoke to her: "You are El-roi [God Sees Me]," for she said, "In this place, have I actually seen the one who sees me?" That is why the well is called Beer-lahai-roi [Well of the Living One Who Sees Me]. It is between Kadesh and Bered.

So Hagar gave birth to Abram's son, and Abram named his son (whom Hagar bore) Ishmael. Abram was eighty-six years old when Hagar bore Ishmael to him. (Gen. 16:7–16)

While traveling in the dry and colorless desert, hopeless and sad, Hagar sat down to rest her swollen belly and quench her thirst with water from a well. We can imagine her, contemplating her circumstances and considering that she should just surrender herself to the desolation and heat of the desert. As we observe her story on the page, the pain of her unseenness is palpable. We feel her losing heart.

But there was One who didn't and wouldn't give up on her, and he made his presence known in her most desperate moment. The angel of the Lord, whom we realize in later verses is God himself, appeared to her. She experienced him as both firm and compassionate: he called her by name and circumstance ("Hagar, slave of Sarai"), gave her specific instructions regarding her circumstance ("Go back"), and promised her a certain future (Through his name, Ishmael, meaning "God hears," her son would be a forever reminder of God's character. He also, through his seed, would become the father of many).

Moments before, Hagar sat dejected by the well. She likely would've died alone in the desert if not for God's intervention. However, the trajectory of her life changed in the second Hagar experienced God as the God who hears and sees. The truth of who he is landed and spread into every crevice of her being, and she immediately broke out in a prayer of joyful thanksgiving and faith, "Truly I have seen the one who looks after me."

Hagar felt seen: known, understood, heard, loved, taken care of, provided for, and protected. The message she received in God's seeing her starkly contrasts with the message of unseenness: she was worthy of love, as was her unborn child.

She marked the most important moment of her life by naming God; and, as a memorial of sorts, she also named the well where he found and rescued her.

All has been made right. Or has it?

Notably, her unique circumstances didn't change. She was still in the desert, still pregnant with Abram's child. And, in fact, the

God Who Sees gave her specific instructions to return home—not to Egypt but to Canaan.

This is difficult to understand, for we know God does not condone abusive behavior or ask us to remain in abusive environments. Rather, God's provision for Hagar would come under the protective umbrella of Abram's lineage.[5] The promise of innumerable offspring both elevated Hagar's status and also ensured her future.[6] Returning would be a matter of obedience but, even more so, a matter of faith.

Hagar knew in her bones that God saw her; and, as deep faith leads us to do, she acted on her belief.

Hagar returned to Abram and Sarai.

Exiting the Desert

Have you ever wondered why God chose to appear to Hagar? Why would he, foreshadowing Elizabeth and Mary and even Sarai herself, make the first-ever birth announcement to a woman we might consider a sideshow in redemptive history? She would not be the mother of the child God promised to Abram. She would not even be in control of her own life. And her son, Ishmael, would go on to torment the chosen child, Isaac. Hagar is not a faultless heroine.

God chose to appear to Hagar because he is a God who acts on what he sees. God didn't just see Hagar; he also *looked upon* his own infallible word, remembering and keeping the covenant he'd made with Abram, as recorded in Genesis 12. Everyone involved

---

5. Genesis 12:1–3.
6. Mathews, *Genesis 11:27–50:26*.

had failed to keep their end of the deal, but God keeps all his promises. He cannot fail to keep his own word. He sees through the lens of his character and promises, and this seeing leads him to act according to that character and those promises. We'll discover specific ways he acts on behalf of those he sees and hears throughout this book; but, for now, we see that Hagar was the blessed recipient of God's rock-solid faithfulness and protection. Because Hagar was carrying Abram's child and because he had promised to bless Abram, he would provide for her and Ishmael.

If God saw and heard one so seemingly insignificant and outside the bounds of his chosen people, how much more does he see us, those belonging to the chosen race[7] through Christ? If he acted on behalf of one whose situation arose from sin, what does that mean for those of us affected by sin, whether deeply wounded by another or experiencing the consequences of our own sin? If he asked Hagar to take difficult steps of faith and obedience in the midst of her pain, what steps of obedience must we take in response to the pain of our unseenness?

In other words, we're not meant to stay in the desert, wallowing in our pain. Exiting the desert starts with hanging our lives on the truth that God sees and acts on what he sees in good and gracious ways. It also means trusting him and acting on our faith through obedience to his instructions.

When I found myself weeping on the counselor's couch, I knew I was, like Hagar, in a desperate place in the wilderness. I didn't know how to get back to life and vitality, but I knew that in my deepest wound the eternal nature of God being a God Who Sees was my balm of comfort.

---

7. 1 Peter 2:9.

Knowing he sees, I could return to my life and live. I could respond in faith and obedience to the instruction God would give, much of which was difficult and beyond my natural capacity—forgiveness, rooting out sin, and embracing being hidden in Christ.[8]

And I did. God has delivered me out of unseenness much like what he did with Hagar. He has met the message I've received of unworthiness with his message of steadfast love. My favorite name of his has become the God Who Sees because he has seen me and has acted on my behalf.

You, too, wherever you are lost and languishing in the desert, can find your way home. That is, in fact, what this book is about. We will walk the steps Hagar walked and discover what Hagar discovered that changed her life and ignited her faith and obedience.

Your journey begins with knowing and believing God has seen and heard everything that's happened to you—every last wound inflicted and every last word spoken.

God is a deeply personal God. He knows you, understands you, hears you, and provides for you. He loves you and wants to be intimately known by you.

In fact, he is so specific and personal that, when the psalmist recalled the way he'd been trampled by others and the way his words had been twisted, he described God recording his misery and storing his tears in a bottle.[9]

Why would God keep accountant-like records of such things?

---

8. Colossians 3:3.
9. Psalm 56:8.

Because every tear over every wound will be met with a specific, detailed redemption. Just as he met Hagar in a way that was uniquely meaningful to her, he demonstrates himself to us in deeply personal ways as a seeing and hearing God.

God is not just *a* seeing and hearing God. He is the God Who Sees—the only God who does.[10]

His seeing is an aspect of his nature and character that sets him apart and demonstrates his glory.

In fact, we would be fools (and our lives will produce the fruit of fools) if we live as if God doesn't see: "Fools, when will you be wise? Can the one who shaped the ear not hear, the one who formed the eye not see?" (Ps. 94:8–9).

The fact that no other god sees or hears makes our God distinct, but it also makes us a distinctive people. We don't have to fear or mourn becoming irrelevant. We don't have to seek visibility through fame, power, or beauty. We don't have to stoke unrighteous anger and unforgiveness as we seek vengeance or vindication. We don't have to fight to be validated by others. We don't need self-affirmation or others' affirmation for our lives to have profound meaning.

What a relief!

What a relief for the despondent in the desert, the hidden and the hiding, the waiters in the wilderness, the wonderers and the wanderers!

You are alive. Look at what you've survived. You are here.

Because someone else is, too.

---

10. Psalm 135:13–18.

For Further Reflection

1. What does it tell you about God that he chose to appear to Hagar in the way he did?

2. In what ways do you feel unseen? Who has made you feel that way?

3. What messages have you received or believed as a result of this unseenness?

4. First Corinthians 13:12 says, "Now I know in part, but then I will know fully, as I am fully known." How is it comforting to you that God knows you fully? Is that scary to you in any way? Explain.

Chapter 2

NAMING UNSEENNESS

We begin our journey out of the desert of unseenness by answering the question for ourselves that God first asked Hagar: "Where have you come from and where are you going?" (Gen. 16:8).

We must note that before he asked her this question, he already knew the answer. He knew where she'd come from and where she intended to go. It seems, then, that the question was primarily for Hagar's benefit. In God's estimation, an important first step for Hagar was hearing herself speak the answer out loud—*I'm running away*—an acknowledgment to God and perhaps to herself of her reality.

Why would God ask Hagar a question he could already answer? Why did he not first offer her comfort, a command, or a truth to consider?

Jesus also often uses this same question-asking tactic in the Gospels in order to reveal his listener's heart *to his listener*. For example, when a rich young man encountered Jesus and asked,

"Good teacher, what must I do to inherit eternal life?," Jesus immediately inquired of him, "Why do you call me good? No one is good except God alone" (Mark 10:17–18). In other words, Jesus asked a question that would reveal what was in his heart: either a belief that he was God and, therefore, an authority on the matter of eternal life or someone unworthy of his belief, submission, and devotion. In the end, the young man's heart was revealed to himself and to all who listened to their exchange: "But he was dismayed by this demand [to turn away from his riches and follow Jesus], and he went away grieving, because he had many possessions" (v. 22).

Similarly, God asked Hagar a question he could already answer himself to reveal her heart to herself, allowing her to see what God already saw inside of her.

But I think there is more to God's question-asking than revealing her heart. When Mark recounts Jesus's interaction with the rich young man mentioned above, he adds a profound, heart-stopping little phrase: "Looking at him, Jesus loved him" (v. 21).

Looking at him, Jesus loved him.

We can imagine the same in God's encounter with Hagar: a looking that was full of love.

When we feel unseen in our difficult circumstances, it's painful when no one asks, when someone asks but doesn't listen, when no one acknowledges our suffering, or when no one acts on what they know. By contrast, a looking from a place of love is one of the most comforting, healing acts in relationships.

In Hagar's story, we see how he worked these two purposes together—using his question both to reveal her heart and to demonstrate that he was aware of her and looking at her from a place of love. This was a pivotal moment, for it's in the intersection of deep need and God's compassionate seeing that one's heart opens itself, as a plant turning toward the sun, receptive to comfort, truth, and direction.

That's exactly what happened in Hagar.

Hagar answered the question asked of her, plainly and honestly. As we know from her subsequent words and actions, she felt seen, heard, acknowledged, and loved. In response, her heart unfolded, a flower before him, malformed and messy from her encounter with malformed and messy humanity—hers and others'.

Hearts unfold like flowers before him.[1] Only then could he show her where he intended for her to be.

Coming and Going

Where have you come from, and where are you going? In our unseenness, the question God asked Hagar is also ours to answer.

Plainly and honestly, letting our hearts reveal themselves. Plainly and honestly, because his looking with love means we can safely reveal ourselves to him.

Where have you come from?

I'll go first, answering as I did that day in the counselor's office.

I've been left behind in church and ministry.

My husband and I moved from Texas to Charlottesville, Virginia, in 2008 to plant a church. Prior to moving, he served

---

1. This familiar phrase originates in Henry Van Dyke's rendition of "The Hymn of Joy," also called "Joyful, Joyful We Adore Thee" (1907).

on a large multistaff church as the college pastor, and since the day we were married, I was happily and heavily engaged in ministry alongside Kyle. In fact, I'd surrendered my life to vocational ministry even before I met him and had attended seminary to prepare. The call to church plant, then, was a shared calling; and, although it was difficult work, I reveled in using my gifts to lead, start the women's ministry, teach the Bible, disciple women, and equip people for the work of ministry. As the church grew, we added staff and elders to the team—a true gift to us and to our church—but I grew increasingly confused about where I fit in as each new person came on board. It was as if we were all on a bus and, with each new addition, I was asked to take a seat further and further away from the action. I happily advocated for those who jumped onto the bus to be given a seat and celebrated and supported them in their ministries. But at some point, it seemed, I'd found myself on the side of the road, watching the bus drive off without me. My husband had gained an incredibly influential role, and I'd worked myself out of a (nonpaying) job.

I'd found my sweet spot and then lost it.

So I raised my hand. I tapped people handing out opportunities on the shoulder and watched others leapfrog to the front of the line. I continued to show up and serve in every way possible; and, if I saw a need, I offered to meet it. I prayed for open doors. I created windows of opportunity for myself and accepted big-C church invitations. But I felt like a has-been at my own church, necessary for the start but excused when the "real" work of ministry began.

And people around me were doing important work, especially my husband. I saw the weight of responsibility he carried as a pastor to many, and I certainly didn't want to add more burdens to his back or be another problem he needed to solve. I wanted to help and support, but I also didn't want to get in the way. I believed I had gifts to offer in service to the church and to Kyle other than smiling and greeting at the door on Sundays as the proper pastor's wife, but because they weren't tapped, I began to question myself. *Perhaps I'm being selfish or prideful. Perhaps I'm falling out of line. Perhaps I want something that is not actually right to want.*

I talked to Kyle about it over and over, and he listened, but he also seemed to think I'd somehow figure it out on my own. But I couldn't figure it out. Somehow Kyle's importance, perspective, job, and needs had become outsized in our marriage; my thoughts, desires, and feelings had come to mean so little.

But that was not all. Around this same time, I'd also been deeply wounded by someone I considered a close friend who showed what I felt was inappropriate interest in my husband. She seemed to desperately want his attention and approval and was willing to hurt me in the process of getting it.

Over many months, alarm bells had started going off, and one of the most jarring alarm bells sent me to her doorstep.

I told her how I felt, not with anger but with many anguished tears. Her response felt inexplicable to me. She was irate—blaming, deflecting, and ultimately refusing to acknowledge my point and my pain. As she was talking, I kept thinking how I would feel or respond if a friend came to me, concerned and hurting because my relationship with her husband felt weird or too familiar. I'd be mortified, apologetic, asking every question I could think of to understand what I'd unintentionally done and what would need to change moving forward to ensure proper boundaries. The contrast was jarring.

Who would listen to my legitimate concerns? Who was willing to protect proper boundaries? Who was willing to consider my feelings?

Where have you come from? This is where: from a place of painful disregard and invisibility.

When I read Hagar's story and observed God inquiring of Hagar, I imagined him inquiring of me; and, in a sense, I saw him seeing me in my suffering. I may have been dismissed by people I loved, but God had his eyes on me. Nothing had occurred outside of his sight.

And where are you going? My response wasn't to run away as Hagar had, but I'd made a home in a pit littered with anger, bitterness, and cynicism. I wasn't going anywhere because I felt stuck, as if nothing could ever change.

Whether I looked at my circumstances from the angle of those who had sinned against me or the angle of my unhealthy responses, I found myself in a desperate, desert place.

Alone and unseen.

Types of Unseenness

Reader, where have you come from, and where are you going? Why do you feel alone in the desert, forgotten, disregarded, or unseen? In other words, what is your reality? And how have you responded to that feeling of unseenness?

Just as God didn't ask Hagar these questions with harsh undertones or folded arms and frustrated sighs, he asks so that your heart might be revealed and that you may experience him seeing you with love and compassion.

If your answer is messy or brutal, tell the God who can handle its weight. If it's laced with tears, let them fall in his presence. If you aren't sure how to put words to the pain, let him translate your groans. Just be honest with yourself and with God because he does his best redemptive work when we acknowledge and live in reality rather than trying to hide.

Scripture invites this type of conversation with God and helps us name the ways we experience unseenness. Naming unseenness out loud to God's listening ear gives voice to our humanity. I dare say it gives voice to the female story in particular; it's no small detail that God was named "the God Who Sees" by a woman. Naming our *specific* unseenness is a breathed invitation for God to hear and layer his *specific* truth like a balm and blanket over us.

Look with me now at the five main categories (and cries) of unseenness we find in Scripture and note which category you most resonate with. We'll dip ever so slightly into some God-oriented truths in this section, but you'll find these categories to be the framework for part 4 of this book.

Being Misunderstood

Sometimes life circumstances can make us feel "other" and leave us feeling misunderstood, even though we may have people in our lives who genuinely try to step into our shoes and understand.

Perhaps you feel invisible or unseen regarding your life circumstances: living as a minority among a majority, caretaking for an elderly parent, navigating a family member's mental illness, or being married to a man with a demanding job. Few know or understand the nuances and intricacies of your specific life circumstance and what burdens you privately carry as a result.

Emily shares her life circumstance that often makes her feel unseen:

> I met and married my ex-husband during seminary, but our marriage ended in divorce because of his unrepentant sin regarding pornography use and infidelity.
>
> I'm now a single mom.
>
> When I first separated from my husband and then divorced him, there was nothing offered at my church for healing or for single-parent families. Although I hated leaving, I needed to find a place where my daughter and I could heal. I found a church that had a single-parent family ministry, an active single adults' group for 30–50's, and Divorce Care for adults and children. I jumped in that church and scoured those groups for single moms who loved Jesus and were trying to love and disciple their kids well. Women of whom I could ask, "How do I do this alone?"
>
> But sometimes I still feel so unseen. For example, my church recently had a parents' night out for only married couples in life groups. Many single moms would love to be included or attend life groups with married couples or families. It gives us safe spaces to ask for help or

advice. It's also good for our kids to be around healthy marriages.

I feel unseen when pastors make statements from the pulpit about private Christian schools or homeschooling being best for kids. As a single working mom, I can't do either, because I can't stay home, and I can't afford private school.

I feel misunderstood when pastors say, "Single moms have the hardest job," and then tell a story about their wife leaving for the weekend and the pastor having to care for the kids alone—getting them to activities and heating up the casserole his wife left. This isn't at all the life of a single mom. My life is filled with endless decisions, worries, financial struggles, preparations for the future, work, and housework, among other things.

Being misunderstood is a category of unseenness most people will fall into at one or more points in their life. Scripture indicates this in Proverbs 14:10: "The heart knows its own bitterness, and no outsider shares in its joy." In other words, you alone can know the nuances of what you experience, whether painful or joyful. This means you can feel misunderstood regarding any circumstance in your life: success or failure, new life or death, dreams fulfilled or losses incurred.

There are many examples in Scripture of a person who is misunderstood. Hannah's anguish in prayer was misunderstood by Eli, the temple priest, as drunkenness (1 Sam. 1:12–14). The apostle Paul was misunderstood and questioned regarding his pastoral choices (2 Cor. 1:15–24), and Jesus himself was misunderstood by not only his enemies but also his own family (Mark 3:21) and friends (Mark 8:31–33; 9:31–32).

Disregard

Disregard is a lack of attention, consideration, or respect. To be disregarded is essentially to be ignored.

Have you felt unseen through disregard? Perhaps you feel invisible because others simply refuse to see you. Maybe, like me, you've disclosed a wound or a need and you've been unheard and rejected. Maybe you've offered a good suggestion or raised your hand at an opportunity and have been ignored. Maybe a friend ghosted you, and you've tried to repair the relationship to no avail. Perhaps you were once cared for in your suffering, but the length of your suffering has made others uncomfortable. You've asked to be seen and have instead been dismissed.

Maybe you've tried to follow all the rules and wait for your turn, and you've looked around and noticed the system is only working for some—primarily those in charge, and you're not in charge. You catch a glimpse of just how invisible you are and just how much righteous pot-stirring would be required to make the system work for everyone. Those in charge aren't intentionally overlooking you; they simply aren't aware that the system isn't working and why it isn't working.

Mackenzie's story is an example of unseenness through disregard:

> When my son, Baylor, died several years ago,
> I felt immediately surrounded by so many.

Family and friends made my husband and me meals, cried when I cried, encouraged me when I allowed myself to feel happy, and allowed me to talk about my son. And then, suddenly it changed. I'm not sure when exactly or why, but people started shifting in their seat when I would bring up my son. When people now ask about my grief, they refer to it in the past tense. In so many ways, I know it's because Baylor's life is past tense to them. That's a normal progression. But, goodness, I feel unseen in my current season. Assuming someone is past their grief, especially one as tragic as losing a child, makes the one grieving feel isolated.

Anna[2] shares how she's felt in her unseenness through disregard:

I've had the privilege of serving my church for almost fifteen years. As with many beginnings, much was required for our local church in infancy. Slowly but surely, the church began to grow and take shape. Along with some faithful friends, I joined the ministry landscape by helping women study their Bibles. What began in our homes grew and eventually moved to the church building, but within our church we existed as a silo of sorts, disconnected from the rest. The leadership would agree that Bible study was a great idea, but

2. Names have been changed.

there was little to no oversight or support. We had to beg to get an announcement included on Sunday morning for Bible study sign-ups or for help with childcare needs.

I began to feel that my contribution as a woman in our church wasn't valued. Since the American church seems to place the highest value on the Sunday sermon, it seems that women are often ignored when it comes to theological or academic input. If a pastor isn't careful, he'll craft his whole lesson, sermon series, and yearly calendar without the feedback of trusted female Bible students and teachers. In spaces of highest leadership, there is a vacuum of female voices, but the women I know that lead have their finger on the pulse of the people in their congregation. They walk with the wounded, provide for the needy, exegete Romans 9, and serve in the nursery. How can the church afford not to hear from them at the highest levels of leadership? The silence is deafening and ultimately hinders the church from embracing the type of partnership the Bible seems to describe.

Whether intentional or unintentional, disregard is painful. David gives voice to this experience in Psalm 31:11–12: "I am ridiculed by all my adversaries and even by my neighbors. I am dreaded by my acquaintances; those who see me in the street run from me. I am forgotten: gone from memory like a dead person— like broken pottery."

Once again, he shifts into hope and trust when he acknowledges that, though his fellow man may avoid him, God sees him and never disregards him:

> I will rejoice and be glad in your faithful love
> because you have seen my affliction.
> You know the troubles of my soul
> and have not handed me over to the enemy. . . .
> But I trust in you, LORD;
> I say, "You are my God."
> The course of my life is in your power;
> rescue me from the power of my enemies
> and from my persecutors. (Ps. 31:7–8, 14–15)

Unfulfilled Desires

We may feel unseen in our desires, specifically our unfulfilled desires. This type of unseenness is often future oriented, fueled by fear, and is, fundamentally, a deep distrust that God cares about what he sees when he sees us.

Perhaps you're single and longing to be married, or you've been praying the same prayer regarding a family member for decades. Perhaps you dream about using your spiritual gifts in a specific way to bless others, but you're currently waiting for God to open doors for you. Perhaps you long for a change in your circumstances.

The prayer of one who feels unseen regarding unfulfilled desires echoes the psalmist who cries, "How long, LORD? Will you forget me forever? How long will you hide your face from me? How long will I store up anxious concerns within me, agony

in my mind every day? How long will my enemy dominate me?"
(Ps. 13:1–2).

Only one who trusts that God is a God Who Sees can wait
with patient hope in the midst of her unfulfilled desires. All the
more incentive to dive into the surefire reasons we can trust God
is a *God Who Sees.*

Injustice

Injustice exists when a wrong has been done and hasn't yet
been righted or reconciled.

Many of the pleading prayers in Scripture come from people
who have been sinned against or who feel the weight of sin's curse
and long for God to make all things right. They feel unseen by
those who've wronged them or those who've sat idly by, allowing
wickedness to prevail. They feel unseen by those who haven't listened or believed them when they've spoken about the injustice.

Perhaps you feel this type of unseenness—an invisibility
in the pain you've endured or witnessed that was caused by the
sins of others. These are the stories we wonder if we can share
with others because we have someone to protect or honor, or we
may be afraid to share because the resulting trauma is difficult
to describe in words and has historically been misunderstood
when we've tried. The shame and disorientation that results from
unseenness through injustice can quickly isolate us, and there's
something deeply lonely about not being able to make those closest to us understand something so pivotal and life defining that's
happened to us.

Niamya[3] tells this kind of story:

> Soon after my husband took his first church staff
> position, the senior pastor cornered me privately
> and made wildly suggestive comments to me.
> I froze, unsure of what to do. If I told, would
> my husband lose his job? Would anyone believe
> me? Had I somehow communicated openness to
> these types of comments? So I remained quiet for
> a long time, not even telling my husband.
>
> I didn't want to go to church. I became closed
> off and guarded. Finally, sensing my withdrawal,
> my husband asked me, "Why are you not sup-
> portive of my ministry?" I broke down and told
> him everything. At first, he didn't believe me,
> which crushed me, but eventually he did and
> then he confronted the pastor. The pastor got
> angry and blamed me. We left the church, but
> it almost destroyed my marriage, and it's com-
> pletely changed my ability to trust people.
>
> My husband took a new job at a different
> church, but I haven't told anyone what happened
> to me. How can I? They wouldn't understand
> how it's affected me, and they might think I am
> somehow to blame. I feel shame about this part
> of my story.

Injustice is, in many senses, both a past and future-oriented
unseenness that tries the human spirit: the godly person must

---

3. Name has been changed.

often navigate a long waiting game for justice while keeping her own heart tender and free from bitterness and anger and her actions free from vengeance, gossip, and slander. The instance or experience of injustice wants to pull us backward, remembering and rehearsing what was done, but the godly must pull forward to the future with the truth that God is just and loves justice.

David gives voice to feeling unseen through an injustice in Psalm 17:2–3: "Let my vindication come from you, for you see what is right. You have tested my heart; you have examined me at night. You have tried me and found nothing evil; I have determined that my mouth will not sin."

His cry to God was for vindication: for the truth to be known, for what's right to win out in the end, and for relationships to be made right. As he wrote this particular psalm, he was still waiting, and his waiting was hopeful, buoyed by his understanding that God sees and acts justly.

Lack of Appreciation

Finally, we can feel unseen in our service to others—taken for granted, taken advantage of, unacknowledged, or devalued. As Christians, we don't serve that we may be seen and appreciated by others (Col. 3:23), but when those receiving benefit from our service don't understand what it's costing us or never acknowledge the benefit they've received, we experience a type of unseenness that can be disheartening.

Perhaps you're a mom who, as the hub of the family wheel, keeps your home and family calendar humming in ways that go unnoticed or unacknowledged. Perhaps you serve in an important yet behind-the-scenes capacity at your church and are wondering if what you do really matters. Perhaps you are trying to do the right thing in a relationship, but the person consistently rejects your prayerfully offered truth and love.

Scripture acknowledges and validates this category of unseenness in the way God relates to the prophets. The prophets, spokesmen for God who were tasked with warning God's people to turn away from their idolatry, are the most unappreciated people in redemptive history. They were called to serve in a way that was meant to be for the life and fruitfulness of the people, but they were roundly despised and rejected because the people didn't want to hear it. Though the prophets literally gave their lives for God's people, they were often callously ignored: "The Lord sent all his servants the prophets to you time and time again, but you have not obeyed or even paid attention" (Jer. 25:4).

One of the prophets, Jeremiah, desperately worried about his people and, therefore, experienced the people's unwillingness to listen as rejection: "But if you will not listen, my innermost being will weep in secret because of your pride. My eyes will overflow with tears, for the Lord's flock has been taken captive" (Jer. 13:17).

Jeremiah encountered deep persecution, but what kept him entrenched in service to the Lord was the knowledge that God sees. When Jeremiah was first called into service as a prophet, God said to him, "I chose you before I formed you in the womb; I set you apart before you were born. I appointed you a prophet to the nations" (1:5). In other words, God saw him long before he was born. This idea—that God sees and acts upon what he sees—sustained Jeremiah when his service to God drew jeers: "Lord of Armies, testing the righteous and seeing the heart and mind, let me see your vengeance on them, for I have presented my case to you" (20:12).

The Common Thread in Unseenness

Whatever story of unseenness you may carry, there is likely a common thread running through it: a message of unworthiness. The unseen wonder if they are worthy of not only being seen but also of being valued. The unseen wonder if it's wrong to want to be seen.

I have many memories as a child of going to the community swimming pool with my parents. My favorite activity at the pool was to perform for my parents; I'd do cannonballs or flips off the diving board, handstands underwater, or choreograph synchronized swimming routines with my sister. After each "performance," I'd turn to my mom or dad and ask for a number rating. My sister and I would compete for the best scores as if we were on the Olympic stage.

More than scores, what I really wanted was my parents' attention. I wanted them to think I did something well, marvel at my skills, or laugh with me over a dive that ended in a belly flop. I wanted to be seen.

Would you say this is a misplaced desire? I don't think so. Every child in every culture is constantly saying, "Mom, watch this!" Or "Dad, look at me!" Instead of a misplaced desire, I would instead call it a God-given desire that images the Godhead. He has made us relational and communal in nature just as he is relational and communal in nature, and our intimacy with him is built on a mutual *seeing*. We're told to taste and *see* that he is good;

he in turn says he *sees* us down to the hairs on our head and in the far reaches of our hearts.

That speaks of infinite worth, bestowed upon us by a God worthy of infinite worship.

Of course, we can set this desire for seenness upon people and instantly distort it into sin and idolatry. So many of our issues in life arise because we think people should respond as only God can (being all-seeing, all-knowing, all-comforting), or because we believe wrongly that God is limited in sight or knowledge or relates to us as some people do: apathetic and disengaged. We must, therefore, always bring our desires for seenness and value to the One who offers both.

God wants us to know we're seen and valued by him; our intimacy with him and delight in him blossoms upon this truth. We will spend much of the rest of this book discovering the nuances and intricacies of how God sees, values, and acts for us based on what he sees. But before we get to the beautiful truths that rise to meet this insidious message of unworthiness, I'm going to ask you to name and sit with me in the pain of your unseenness.

There is an invitation for you in the pain: an invitation to a profound and personal intimacy with him, a peace with whom he's created us individually to be, and the ability to be fully present and visibly vulnerable in relationships with others.

Don't you want that in whatever ways unseenness is woven into the fabric of your story?

Only then can he show us where he intends for us to be or to go. *Where have we come from, and where are we going?*

We may have come from pain, but we're going forward with the God Who Sees.

For Further Reflection

1. Where have you come from? Where are you going?

2. What are your primary categories of unseenness? God sees your circumstances. God records your tears. What are the reasons for your tears?

3. How have you responded to feelings of unseenness?

4. How does it help you to know that your desire to be seen by God is one he wants to meet?

Chapter 3

THE PAIN OF UNSEENNESS

As we return to Hagar in the desert, we recognize that there is an undercurrent of emotion in her story. Her story's scaffolding is framed with the facts like the wood and nails of a structure, but the emotions of the story fill in the fine details like paint color and furniture.

What emotional words appear in Hagar's story in Genesis 16?

> *Contempt* (v. 4): When Hagar became pregnant, she began treating Sarai with disrespect and disdain. Sarai reported this dishonor to Abram.

> *Mistreated* (v. 6): Scripture, as an outside observer, reports that Sarai mistreated Hagar. Though Hagar didn't describe her emotions around this mistreatment, we can certainly imagine she felt harmed, misused, and wronged.

> *Afflicted* (v. 11): Notably, God himself named Hagar's specific pain in her specific unseenness.

He said, "The LORD has heard your *cry of affliction*" (emphasis added). I love this about God,
that he reflected to her what he observed, essentially saying, "In all of your hardship, misery, and
torment, I've watched your tears fall, and I've
heard the need in your groans."

We can feel the pain emanating from these particular pages
of Scripture, and it's difficult to sit with. But we're exploring the
emotional arena of the story because it's not enough to simply
name the facts of our unseenness or to intellectually know the
name and character of God. To experience the life-giving truth
and healing balm of encountering the God Who Sees as Hagar
did, we must also spend time considering the undercurrent of
emotions in our unseenness and how God meets us there.

We must pay attention to our own cry of affliction.

When my counselor helped me name my deepest wound
of being unseen, it was as if my life suddenly made sense to me
after years of groping in the dark. Looking through this filter, I
regarded my relationships, my choices and frustrations, my ambi-
tions and desires, and even my dreams from a new angle. I saw
myself, perhaps for the first time, with compassion.

In response to my cry of affliction, the counselor sat with me
for a moment and then gently whispered, "When we awaken to
reality, we weep."

Yes, I suppose so, but I do not like to cry a cry of affliction, especially in front of others, so my natural inclinations and
defenses instantly kicked in—anything to quell the weeping.

Characteristically, my immediate inclination was to reach for
an action plan. *What do I do? How do I attack this problem? What*

is the formula or algorithm for unlocking the answer to this puzzle? Where is the express clinic so I might quickly bind up this wound? I wanted to get moving so I didn't have to feel sad.

Then my theological training kicked in, Bible verses standing at the ready, first, to convince me the desire to be seen by others is prideful and selfish and, second, to remind me of the truths I should believe instead. If I just mentally assented to these truths, surely the difficult feelings would disappear. This was an attractive defense because I wanted to stay out of the emotional arena entirely.

My final defense, victimhood, silently and patiently waited its turn but soon began to whisper under its breath, telling me who deserved blame for my hurt and how exactly I could lord it over them. I didn't want to take responsibility for my healing but rather make it the responsibility of others. I wanted to be angry so I didn't have to feel sad.

Going with the first tactic (and my lifelong inclination), I dabbed with a tissue at my tears, sat up straight, and asked, "So, what do I do?"

"You sit with the pain," he replied.

I sank back down into the couch cushion. Rebellion against the counselor rising in my chest, I thought, *What good does it really do me to see and name this wound, much less sit in the pain of it?*

Are Emotions Bad?

Perhaps you're asking the same question. Like me, you can pinpoint the ways you feel unseen and want to either jump immediately to biblical truths and action steps or wallow in victimhood, savoring your bitterness. Why give space to the emotional arena in our exploration of God being the God Who Sees? After all, if we've heard it once, we've heard it a thousand times: the heart can't be trusted. Our emotions don't speak truth.

We start in the emotional arena because that's where our humanity naturally takes us when we initially experience pain. God has designed us this way. Like a finger burned by fire, the jolt of pain tells us that something isn't right; the singe tells us to immediately seek our well-being, protection, and healing away from the fire.

In other words, we start in the emotional arena because in the pain of being unseen lies an invitation to first seek refuge and comfort and, afterward, to find our marching orders. The invitation is to acknowledge to ourselves that something in our lives is not right or not working, to experience God as the God Who Sees in that circumstance, and then, like Hagar, to follow God's leading out of the desert through faith and obedience.

I think of the apostle Paul, also called Saul, and his fateful encounter with the risen Jesus on the road to Damascus. At times, I've wondered why God blinded Saul and then left him blind for three days. In those blackened hours, Saul only knew that Jesus had appeared to him and asked, *Why?* "Saul, Saul, why are you persecuting me?" (Acts 9:4).

Saul sat with that question for three long days. Imagine the range of emotions he experienced. He didn't eat or drink throughout his ordeal, which indicates a frailty of spirit, a deep grief over what he'd done, or perhaps grave and stunned amazement at encountering someone he'd built his life around hating. We can imagine his incredible sense of disorientation and failure as he

reflected on his life choices considering what he'd come to understand was true. Maybe he was embarrassed that his fellow travelers
had heard him rebuked. Or perhaps he felt fearful as he wondered
how God might deal with him next or how he'd live the rest of his
life as a blind man.

What was the invitation for Saul in those three days and all
that uncertainty, godly sorrow, and discomfort?

It's the same invitation that awaits us in our pain of unseenness: the invitation to a new way of life. What if, like Saul, sitting
with our pain and exploring it is the way we see and choose a new
way of life? What if it's the way to growth and change? What if
it's a bridge toward intimacy with God and perhaps, if wise, even
those who've sinned against us? What if it's even the pathway to
more purposeful and joy-filled living?

But emotion remains a bad word for many of us. If ever we
hear, "She's emotional," we automatically intuit "she" is a problem
to solve. We tend to overvalue our intellect and undervalue our
emotions because emotions have been deemed dangerous: they
are a slippery slope to losing control or allowing our feelings to
overrule truth.

Let's start with the truth, then. What does the Bible teach us
about emotions?

First, God himself is an emotional being. Throughout
Scripture, we discover that he demonstratively feels joy and delight
(Zeph. 3:17), grief (Eph. 4:17), anger and wrath (Matt. 21:12–13;
Rom. 1:18), sorrow (John 11:32–35), jealousy (Exod. 34:14), love
(1 John 4:10), amazement (Mark 6:5–6), anguish (Matt. 26:36–
46), betrayal (Matt. 26:47–50, 69–75), and compassion (Luke
7:12). He laughs, he cries, and he lets loose on his enemies.

Second, God created us as emotional beings, and he created the emotions we feel. From the beginning of time in the garden of Eden, we gather that Adam and Eve felt delight in God, pleasure in each other, and satisfaction and peace in doing the work God had given them.

As image bearers, then, we image God in and through our rightly ordered emotions. Grief and sadness are right responses to pain and death. Gladness is a right response to receiving encouragement. Righteous anger is warranted in the face of injustice or sin. Jealousy is a right response to a marriage boundary crossed. Joy is a right response to sins made white as snow.

Every emotion we have was created and given to us by God. He didn't just create what we term the "positive" emotions. Yet we too often divide emotions into "positive" and "negative" categories and believe, as Christians, we're required to stay within the "positive" emotional arena. However, no emotion is right or wrong, positive or negative—although some are harder to feel than others, and, of course, they can be taken to sinful extremes.

Regarding our emotions, what is a sinful extreme? In *Gentle and Lowly*, Dane Ortlund writes, "Fallen emotions not only sinfully overreact; they also sinfully under-react."[1] Sinful overreaction allows emotions to rule and reign, where sadness becomes hopeless despair, loneliness becomes anger at others, or uncertainty becomes anxiety. By contrast, sinful underreaction shuts emotions off entirely—a type of numbing of the self—keeping us, for example, from mourning with those who mourn or rejoicing with

---

1. Dane Ortlund, *Gentle and Lowly* (Wheaton, IL: Crossway Books, 2020), 107.

those who rejoice.[2] When we numb ourselves, we fail to acknowledge and name our own emotions, remaining unaware of our own selves. And emotional self-awareness is a necessary ingredient of connection and intimacy with God and others.

Emotions as Opportunities

Our emotions, especially the more difficult ones, act as both a signal and an invitation.

Have you ever been driving along on the highway and a light starts flashing on your dashboard? Maybe a tire has low air pressure, or your tank is low on gas. The lights on the car dashboard are designed to warn you that, one, something is wrong and, two, a specific action is needed in response.

Emotions act like signals in the same way. They act as an opportunity for us to see and acknowledge what may be going on in the "engine" or the heart.

Just as we would look under the hood of the car when lights on the dashboard start blinking, emotions are signals that we should examine our hearts. What evidence do these specific emotions provide regarding our heart's allegiance? Is it to Christ? Then the Bible says we will experience increasing peace and joy despite any difficult circumstances we face. But if it is not to Christ; if it is to a child, reputation, belonging, or appearance, for example, anytime that allegiance feels threatened, we will experience a flair of reactive responses like stress, anger, despair, control, self-isolation, or self-protection.

---

2. Romans 12:15.

These are the lights on the dashboard, telling us that we're protecting and defending an idol.

I want to be clear that not all "negative" emotions represent idolatry. The point is that we must examine our emotions to see what's underneath the hood, so to speak.

Emotions are signals, but they are also *invitations* for, as we've already established, connection and intimacy.

Consider for a moment what happens when a close friend shares a part of her heart with you and when you share yours with her. Perhaps it's a moment of confessing sin or asking for help or sharing a vulnerable story. It's a moment pregnant with emotion. What happens in that moment? Connection and intimacy happen. Relational closeness happens. Mutually sharing on an emotional or spiritual level builds and cements a friendship.

The same is true in our relationship with God. Consider what could happen when you experience something exciting or something difficult, and instead of numbing that feeling, you acknowledge it to yourself and then name it to him? It builds relational intimacy between you and God.

Our spiritual health is not solely based on knowing Scripture. It's also based on experiencing the God that Scripture talks about in a personal and intimate way, and intimacy with God happens at the emotional level.

As Christians, we must know that truth and emotions are not enemies; in fact, they work in harmony and are cyclical. Truth invites emotions, and emotions, if rightly handled, are an invitation to truth, which leads us to respond emotionally.

Specific Emotions Invite Specific Truth

In the last chapter, we named the specific types of unseenness we may experience. Now, we must name the specific emotions that accompany these experiences.

Let's first acknowledge that many of us are not skilled at naming our emotions. I find it helpful to keep a list of emotions (see Appendix A) handy for times such as these. Like a liturgy, when I don't have words for my cry of affliction, I'm given the words. And when I can only think of general categories of emotions, the list helps me get more specific with myself and with God.

What is the specific pain you feel in being unseen? (Use the words I've given you if you need help.)

Perhaps you feel a deep sense of loneliness or isolation. You are certain you can only rely on yourself.

Perhaps you feel the frustrating tension of living under the expectations or standards that others have of who you should be and what you should do but then experiencing their lack of approval when you try to obey the Lord instead.

Perhaps you feel anger at being controlled rather than allowed to be who God has made you to be.

Perhaps you feel shame over labels you've carried since your childhood that have mischaracterized you or shown that others have misunderstood you: "the ugly one" or "the fighter" or "the problem child."

Perhaps you feel disregarded because a relational rupture hasn't been repaired and your side of the story was never asked for, heard, or believed.

Perhaps you feel taken for granted because you make your home or workplace hum, but no one seems to notice, and no one offers thanks but rather offers grumbling and complaining.

Probably, you feel unworthy to be seen, heard, listened to, learned from, celebrated, or loved.

How do these emotions, rightly handled, invite truth? When we take them to God, we can cast our specific care on him, as Scripture teaches us to do.[3] And then, as we present ourselves to him, he "casts" truth back to us through his Word regarding that specific care.

We find that God never disregards his children but instead hears their cries and responds to their requests (Ps. 116). We find that he himself was rejected and despised and, therefore, can sympathize with our feelings (Isa. 53:3–4; Heb. 4:14–16). We find that he takes note of all we do in his name, even if it's hidden from the eyes of others (Matt. 6:6; Heb. 6:10). These truths, when meditated on, digested, and believed, invite new emotions to replace the old: comfort, peace, reassurance, and gratefulness. We're safe in him.

Truth invites emotions, and emotions invite truth. And the more specific we get with God, the better. Consider, for example, when someone you love offers you a compliment. If he or she says, "You look nice today," you certainly appreciate the compliment, but the vagueness is like tape with little stick left—it falls off of you quickly. But what if he or she says, "That shirt really makes your eyes pop. That shade of blue is definitely your color!" The specificity makes the compliment more memorable and meaningful. When you see that shirt hanging in your closet, you'll

---

3. 1 Peter 5:7.

remember with fondness the words of encouragement, and you'll likely choose to wear that shirt much more often than before!

So it is with God. Rather than expressing a vague unsettledness (or not expressing an emotion to him at all), we must consider the exact type of emotion we're feeling and share it with him. Is it sadness? What specific sort of sadness? Is it boredom? What specific sort of boredom? Is it shame? What specific sort of shame? As we get to the specifics of what we're feeling, we can more specifically and personally come to know God, the many facets of his character, and how he responds to us.

My go-to response to difficult emotions like sadness or loneliness is to immediately *do something*. I can attack anything with a to-do list or checklist. It's as if I believe that as soon as I learn the lesson God has for me, I can get through whatever is hard. Or if I just do certain steps in a certain way, I can shorten the suffering. But in the long season of unseenness, I experienced such deep suffering that I realized I can't act my way out of painful emotions. Instead, I began to see them as invitations from God to walk with him in it. I had to get over the idea that my painful emotions are shameful, and I had to stop berating myself with what I *should* think and feel, as if I should be farther along already.

I began a practice of naming my emotions as specifically as possible to God using the list of emotions I've given you in Appendix A. And then, as specifically as possible, I name attributes of God that apply to my emotions (see Appendix B) or truths from Scripture that speak to that emotion. (I keep both lists in my Bible, handy for prayer and meditation.) As I made this a practice, I began experiencing emotion and truth working together like two hands. I would say to God, "I feel hurt today over how my friend so deeply wounded me and won't acknowledge what I've tried to tell her. I want vindication and the truth to be known." Looking over the list of attributes, God would remind me that he is just and that he alone judges and vindicates perfectly, so I could leave it in his hands. It was both a sense of conviction to release vindication into his hands and a balm of comfort that God heard my cries and received my requests.

David's Journal Entry

Let's look together at a biblical example of this practice, specifically in the life of King David.[4] In a long period of unseenness, David exemplified how emotion invites truth and truth invites emotion.

As a young man, long before he was king, David was a shepherd boy. One day, called in from the fields, he found Samuel, the priest of Israel, standing in his living room. David didn't yet know it, but God had revealed to Samuel that he'd rejected the current king of Israel, Saul, and had provided a new one for himself. David also didn't yet know that Jesse, his father, had already paraded David's seven older brothers before Samuel, and none had been confirmed as the future king. As a last-ditch effort, Jesse had sent for David.

When Samuel saw David, he also heard God say, "Anoint him, for he is the one" (1 Sam. 16:12). When he did so, the Spirit of the Lord rushed upon David.

---

4. You can read about this part of David's life in detail starting in 1 Samuel 16 and continuing through the end of 2 Samuel.

It was clear to all present, including David himself, through this unique experience and anointing, that David would one day replace Saul as king.

But Saul was still alive and still the reigning king.

Soon after, as Providence would have it, Saul met David. Saul had become mentally disturbed and found that music soothed him. David, adept at playing music, attended Saul, comforting him with his instrument.

Initially, Saul and David had a good relationship, but one day Jesse sent David with food for his brothers. They were on the front lines of a battle between Israel and the Philistines. Instead of leaving the food and returning home, David grew curious and went toward the action. He saw for himself what the Israelites were up against: a huge giant of a man named Goliath had come forward from the Philistines to taunt the Israelites. David felt sure he could kill Goliath, so he went to Saul and asked permission to fight him. Saul gave it.

As we well know, David killed Goliath, and that one victory changed his entire life. He became instantly famous and was celebrated by his people, but the one who'd loved and trusted him—King Saul—became immediately threatened and jealous over David's growing influence and celebrity, so much so that he concocted a plan to kill David.

David fled the palace, heading into the wilderness, moving from cave to cave as Saul and the king's men hunted him.

How long did this cat-and-mouse game continue? Scholars say the gap of time between Samuel anointing David and David becoming king was about ten years. For ten years, David knew what God intended for him but had no idea how it would come to be. For ten years, David lived under the reign of one who could control the entire narrative. For ten years, David faced a death sentence.

And amid those stressors, he lost a best friend and a wife, and he was misunderstood and challenged by his own men.

Could David have felt unseen and alone? Could he have wondered why God was allowing these events to unfold? Did he experience pain because of the sin of someone else? Certainly.

However, we must note that in the midst of his unseenness, he was able to respond to his circumstances in ways that are not natural human responses: he spared Saul's life twice rather than take revenge or force his way into his promised role. He persuaded others to spare Saul's life. He promised Saul he wouldn't cut off Saul's offspring when he became king. He seemed to hold no bitterness in his heart toward Saul, and he trusted God to protect him and ascend him to the throne.

How did he do this? I think it had everything to do with the combination of his spiritual and emotional health. We can peek into his journals, as it were, to discover an emotionally adept man. Repeatedly, throughout his poems and songs, we see how his emotions invited truth, and the truth about God settled his emotions.

Following is an example of one his journal entries, written when he was on the run from Saul and one that provides us a pattern to follow in the emotions of our own unseenness. Notice the title and how similarly it corresponds with God's acknowledgment of Hagar's emotional distress, and see if you resonate with what David expresses.

Psalm 142: A Cry of Distress

A *Maskil* of David. When he was in the cave.
A prayer.

I cry aloud to the LORD;
I plead aloud to the LORD for mercy.
I pour out my complaint before him;
I reveal my trouble to him.
Although my spirit is weak within me,
you know my way.
Along this path I travel
they have hidden a trap for me.
Look to the right and see:
no one stands up for me;
there is no refuge for me;
no one cares about me.

I cry to you, LORD;
I say, "You are my shelter,
my portion in the land of the living."
Listen to my cry,
for I am very weak.
Rescue me from those who pursue me,
for they are too strong for me.
Free me from prison
so that I can praise your name.
The righteous will gather around me
because you deal generously with me.

Let's ask these questions of the text:

> *What did David feel or experience?*
>
> *What did David do as a result of what he felt or experienced?*
>
> *Whom did David say God was and is?*

Let's start with exploring David's emotions: What did he feel? He described feelings of desperation, of being troubled and trapped, of weakness and helplessness, and of feeling completely alone. Notice how specifically he described his emotions, how attuned he was to what was happening inside himself.

In light of David's emotions, what did he do? He cried out to the Lord, pouring out his complaints and telling God about his troubles. In other words, he examined his emotions and let them lead him to God, the Source of comfort and truth.

His specific emotions then invited specific truth about God: he is merciful, omniscient ("you know my way"), generous, a refuge, and a deliverer.

Finally, David made requests of God based on God's character. He asked God to act as the merciful and generous Deliverer that he is.

By the end of the psalm, we glimpse David's settled and hopeful heart as he imagines a future moment when he could tell those gathered around him about how exactly God had delivered him.

David's emotions invited truth, and truth invited his emotional response.

And what happened in the process?

David's relational connection with God was strengthened.

And though still alone in the cave, David knew he wasn't. He knew he was seen by God.

You, too, can follow the pattern of David's life as you navigate unseenness, experiencing through this practice being seen by God. Ask yourself:

> *What do I feel?* Use the list of emotions at the back of the book if you need help.

> *What will I do?* Follow David's lead and go to God to tell him how you feel and receive his truth.

> *What do I know about God that speaks to my experience and that I will call upon?* Use the attribute list at the back of the book if you need help.

> *What specific requests does that lead me to make of God?* In other words, how do you want him to act according to his attributes and nature?

God Does His Best Work in Reality

What I'm saying with all this talk about emotion—which is what I believe Scripture is saying—is that the way to hope and joy in unseenness is to deal in reality: the reality of our specific pain, rather than trying to ignore or resist it; the reality that something isn't right, rather than trying to talk yourself out of it or letting others talk you out of it; and the reality that God wants to meet you in a deeply personal way in your unseenness because he is a deeply personal God.

God deals in reality; he does his best work when we're honest with him about what we're facing.

Do you see this sort of invitation in your own pain of unseenness?

I know—it's a difficult invitation to accept. Rather than an invitation to growth, we'd much prefer clear answers to the questions clanging around in our hearts and minds: *Where were you, God? Do you see what is happening to me, God? Can I trust you, God? Does it even matter what I'm doing for you, God?* These, too, are questions about reality—about the human experience—so we are safe to ask these questions of God, and we will in later chapters.

Perhaps you see the invitation, but you're not sure you can trust him with your wounds. Perhaps you're somewhere in the in-between, peering longingly back at what was (what now feels lost) and coaxing yourself to accept God's outstretched hand as he gestures forward.

When I was deeply wounded from being unseen and disregarded and asking all the questions, my faith felt small. I'd been rattled, and I found myself trembling when I wanted instead to be confident in God.

So I stood, paralyzed, not sure if I should look back and spend time grieving the loss of what was good or looking ahead for a better day.

I finally realized that I was trying to avoid plunging into darkness. I didn't want to grieve properly what felt sad because, well, I didn't want to feel sad. (Who likes to feel sad?) And I didn't want to step forward because, although the present day felt doable, what if the future wasn't doable? What if more heartache and loss awaited?

Do you, too, feel this fear?

In *A Grace Disguised*, Jerry Sittser says, "The quickest way to reach the sun and the light of day is not to run west, chasing after the setting sun, but to head east, plunging into the darkness until one comes to the sunrise."[5]

I didn't, of course, want to face loss. I'd much rather have "chase[d] the setting sun," attempting to prevent darkness and the effects of loss, or trying to get back what once was, which was just delusion.

But I liked the thought of a sunrise dawning after what felt at the time like an endless night. I liked it because it reminded me of my Morning Star (Rev. 22:16).

He waited for me, walking at my pace. He was gentle with me. He spoke tenderly to me in the dark, calling me forward to more of him and more of who I'm meant to be.

He waits for you, too.

Chasing the setting sun rejects and resists how God might want to change you. But plunging willingly into the uncertainty of the darkness he's written into your story, looking for the sunrise, is like saying into the night, "Here I am, Lord. Whatever it takes, make me wholly yours."

Or as Eugene Peterson says, "We don't have to eliminate pain to have joy—it's a futile strategy. All suffering, all pain, all emptiness, all disappointment is seed: sow it in God and he will, finally, bring a crop of joy from it."[6]

---

5. Jerry Sittser, *A Grace Disguised* (Nashville: Zondervan, 1995), loc. 405.

6. Eugene Peterson, *A Long Obedience in the Same Direction* (Grand Rapids, MI: InterVarsity Press, 2021), loc. 823.

He's done that for me in the pain of my unseenness. I sowed in the darkness, but I chose to sow it in God. He's used the reality of my specific pain to reveal himself to me and change me in a specific way.

I want the same for you. I want to hold your hand and take you to God and show you that he is a God Who Sees you in such a specific, personal, intimate way that it changes everything.

Will you sow your suffering in him and let him bring you a crop of joy?

Then reach for his outstretched hand.

For Further Reflection

1. Aside from the emotions listed in the chapter, what emotions does God display in Scripture?

2. What is the specific emotion you feel regarding your unseenness? Use the words listed in Appendix A to help you. Follow David's example: go to God and tell him how you feel.

3. What do you know about God from Scripture that speaks to your specific experience and emotion? What characteristic about God can you call upon in your pain? Use Appendix B for help.

4. What specific requests does knowing these things about God lead you to pray?

5. Now that you've named your specific pain, what would happen if you didn't minimize it but instead paid attention to it? What

could happen if you didn't shove the feelings aside and explored them instead? What might open to you if you asked, "What's the invitation for me here in the pain of my unseenness?"

Part Two

HIDING

Chapter 4

HIDING IN PLAIN SIGHT

We've spent so much time sitting with Hagar, but there is another unseen woman in Genesis 16, and we have much to learn from her as well.

Sarai.

Sarai desperately wanted a baby. In a world where a woman's significance rested in marriage and childbirth, her infertility surely buried her into the shadows of the daily rhythms of her community. Worse, in her culture, barrenness was considered shameful—a sure sign of God's angry withholding. Could she have felt misunderstood, overlooked, and disregarded?

While Hagar, the unseen woman, ran away from her circumstances, Sarai, the unseen woman, took control of her circumstances. Distrusting that God would see and act on his promises, Sarai fought for her own seenness and worth in her community through her acts of independence and self-sufficiency. According to her own careful plans, she would move the hand of God.

Notice the distrust lurking beneath Sarai's explanation to Abram regarding her actions: "Since the LORD has prevented me from bearing children, . . ." (Gen. 16:2). The Lord, she said, had *prevented* her—stopped her, withheld from her. In her calculations, God had not kept his promise to her, so she'd decided to act for herself.

Had the Lord actually prevented her? *Yes.* She hadn't yet had a child. She legitimately had an unmet desire, a longing. Day after day, she stared at an unfulfilled promise. Her life was not how she'd planned it to be, not by a long shot. We can certainly imagine that she felt unseen and desperate.

We can also imagine that her longing elicited grief, and grief is not in itself a distrust of God. Grief and hope can go hand in hand.

However, in the pain of unseenness, she didn't run to God; she took matters into her own hands, attempting to force a solution or resolution to her pain. Her solution was to insert herself into the place of God's authority.

Sarai made the wound of her longing to be seen into a weapon that hurt others and, in turn, hurt herself.

Seeking seenness apart from God may seem appealing and may even be successful and satisfying for a time, but it always leads to dark, lonely places—to even deeper unseenness.

I know something about that.

Because I am Sarai.

In the ensuing months of "sitting with the pain" of my own unseenness, anger quickly replaced my sadness. I was, first and foremost, angry at myself. How could I have allowed myself to go unseen for so long? Why had I explained away yellow and red flags in my friendship to my own detriment and her benefit? When had I decided that my preferences and needs in marriage were meant to be muted?

I was angry with my friend, and the anger only grew when it became clear she would never acknowledge how she'd hurt me. I was also angry at Kyle for not listening to me and repeatedly invalidating my concerns and desires. But I felt betrayed and confused in ways that seemed inordinately larger than the facts of the situation.

I had trouble making sense of this.

Why, I asked my counselor, *is it okay for people to treat me however they want?*

That's where I felt I was: living in a boundary-less place where others could trample in and out as they pleased, blissfully unaware of what it all was costing me, happily apathetic toward what I thought and felt and wanted.

I'd always thought of myself as a strong, independent woman—a visible go-getter, decisive and discerning, not a doormat, not someone ruled by fear or quick to blow past yellow flags.

But as I wrestled and puzzled and struggled my way through the ensuing months, I began to see myself differently: I hadn't merely gone unseen by people I loved.

I had *contributed* to my own unseenness. I had taken matters into my own hands, trying to be seen in all the wrong ways.

I'd been hiding in plain sight practically my whole life.

Strategies to Be Seen

As we all do, I learned at any early age what was expected of me. I learned what adults and authority figures valued and honored and what they didn't value and honor. And I learned what they most appreciated in and about me. So I did the things that earned me their praise.

I also learned what elicited negative responses. Vulnerable feelings weren't welcomed or modeled, so I learned early on to keep myself under strict guard. If I took the risk of expressing my need for comfort or my preferences that stood in contrast to what was expected, I felt dismissed in ways that made me feel bad for having them. So, easily enough, I refrained from doing the things that earned me all risk and little reward: sharing my thoughts, feelings, questions, preferences, desires, or hurts.

Like Sarai, I learned self-sufficiency. And self-sufficiency offered me a type of seenness.

In other words, I developed a strategy for acceptance and validation, and I quickly excelled at that strategy. I went hard after what earned praise, and anything that didn't, I tucked away under lock and key. I didn't know I was honing a strategy, nor did I understand what result I was working that strategy for, but I became an expert at it.

That strategy was performance: being a "good" girl, excelling at sports and academics, moving into leadership in whatever organization, group, or club I chose to participate in, and striving to be successful in everything I did. My strategy even bled over into my walk with Jesus: I made it my goal to perform well for him through perfectly practiced spiritual disciplines, carefully cultivated self-grown spiritual fruit (as if there is such a thing), and impeccable behavior.[1]

---

1. Thankfully, in my twenties, the Lord broke me of this strategy, specifically in my relationship with him. I wrote about it in my book, *From Good to Grace*. I didn't know vestiges of it remained in my relationships with others.

I legitimized myself through success. I sought value through doing.

Through performance, I earned visibility and, through visibility, praise, and that praise felt warm, like a blanket of security and safety and belonging. It felt like love.

So what my strategy earned me became like a drug. I could, in a sense, push a certain button and receive an instant hit: a moment when I would be seen and celebrated, perhaps even admired or marveled at, a moment that inoculated me for a time from the constant certainty and fear I was disappointing everyone around me. (Because one can never perform well enough; there is always a new bar to reach for, a new person to not disappoint, an evolving expectation to meet.)

Unlike illicit drug use, my strategy was acceptable. More than acceptable, it was prized—at school, at church, at work, and at home.

So I pushed that button over and over and over again. And it worked over and over and over again. I even came to define myself according to my strategy: capable and successful and independent, and, yes, self-sufficient. Very self-sufficient.

However, I had no awareness that, below the surface, each push of the button was watering a creeping vine that, year by year, inched closer to the heart of who I am. The creeping vine planned to wrap its way around my heart, to steal, kill, and destroy,[2] to take every inch of vitality I had and replace it with pride, self-loathing, hard-heartedness, and bitterness.

When I developed a strategy for being seen and validated, a dual life was born. I learned to hide some things, and I don't mean

---

2. John 10:10.

just sinful things, but also things about myself that I'd learned were unacceptable to those who doled out the praise. Sometimes the unacceptable thing was my opinion or idea. Sometimes it was my preference. Sometimes it was part of my personality that didn't fit what was expected. Sometimes it was my hurt or struggle that I knew, if shared, would be dismissed. Sometimes it was my need for help or assurance or encouragement. Sometimes it was the overwhelming feeling that I couldn't keep up with what was expected of me.

Always, I hid the most vulnerable parts of me from even the closest people in my life. I learned, in a sense, never to make the mistake again of sharing my honest thoughts and emotions because to do so was to open myself up to condemnation and shame. Instead, I leaned heavily on the acceptable parts and found that the more I pushed the button, the greater the distance I could maintain from the unacceptable parts. In fact, I started believing what others said or implied about those vulnerable parts: I was bad. I was wrong. I was to blame. I was too much while simul- taneously not enough. I should never trust my own thoughts, perspectives, and emotions. I could not trust others because they only valued me for what I could do for them.

I have carried these messages with me into every relation- ship I've ever been in, always questioning myself, always sure I'm disappointing.

And of course, the kicker is that I had no idea all of this was happening under the surface of my life. I had no idea how much I was hiding in plain sight until I'd pushed the button enough times that the vine had wrapped tightly around my heart and started squeezing. The real me, with real feelings and thoughts and preferences and needs, was suffocating, and I had learned to call it normal and self-denial and being a pastor's wife and being a mom and being human.

I'd taught people it was okay to disregard me with a dazzling sideshow of success.

Like Sarai, I wanted to blame my friend, and I wanted to blame Kyle, but part of my suffering was a mess of my own making. Before I could see the circumstances clearly or diagnosis the speck in others' eyes, I first needed to dislodge the log in my own.[3]

The First Strategy

My story and Sarai's story should sound familiar because it's the story of being human.

Our first parents, Adam and Eve, walked peacefully and joyfully in the garden with God, fully known by him and by one another and fully knowing him and one another. The sin we now know like the air we breathe, they didn't yet know. They didn't feel any urge to hide. They didn't know feelings of condemnation, shame, anger, or sadness resulting from distorted thinking and broken relationships.

But when they ate of the forbidden fruit, "the eyes of both of them were opened, and they knew they were naked" (Gen. 3:7). Prior to her first bite, we learn that Eve "saw that the tree was good for food and delightful to look at, and that it was desirable for obtaining wisdom" (v. 6). She wanted to see as God alone can see, to know as God alone can know. Adam joined her in her

---

3. Matthew 7:3.

desire, and their desire to see, when acted upon, instead veiled their sight.

The aftershocks of their disobedience were immediate: a realization of the existence of sin, shame, fear, blame, deflection. A rift between husband and wife—a deep loneliness—and a rift between the created and their Creator—an even deeper sadness.

What did they do? "They knew they were naked; so they sewed fig leaves together and made coverings for themselves" (v. 7). They felt shame and vulnerability, so they hurried to hide themselves from being fully seen and known, only allowing each other and God to see what they, in their distorted vision, deemed their presentable parts.

Who had, for that singular moment, had his way? The serpent had. The creeping vine immediately multiplied, spreading into every human heart.

And he's had his way in every moment since when we, too, reach for a fig leaf in the aftermath of sin (ours or others against us) to cover our own vulnerability and shame and be found presentable to ourselves and others. He's had his way when we've found identity in our fig leaves, getting too good at hiding ourselves from being vulnerably seen and known. He's had his way when we, like Eve and like Sarai, grasp to be God and to make our own way through our strategies.

Eve wanted to see like God. Sarai wanted to be seen by God in her predetermined way.

This is our story. Every person has a strategy that we employ to see and be seen because every human being desires validation and acceptance. One cursory glance at the world around you and you'll start to recognize various strategies popping up everywhere.

In fact, most of what we see in the news stems from some action or advocacy taken as a result of someone either wanting to feel seen or someone who feels unseen and is trying—many times desperately—to change that.

Consider the declining professional sports star who can't walk away from the game into anonymity.

Consider the woman who has gained attention and accolades because of her appearance, so as she ages, she spends countless hours and dollars on beauty treatments, plastic surgery, styling sessions, and photoshopping pictures for the Internet.

Consider the constant push in our culture toward identity politics, diversification, and representation. People are shouting to be seen for the unique individual they are or for their unique sexuality, and they get riotously angry when they feel underrepresented or overlooked.

Consider the isolated teenage boy who goes on a shooting rampage in order for his name to be known and written in the history books.

Consider the politician who wants to keep his name in the news and will do and say anything to that end.

Being successful, beautiful, popular, famous, or representing your heritage well isn't the problem. Similarly, the desire for love, validation, and acceptance is not inherently bad; it's the *striving* and *seeking* to be seen by our fellow human beings that malform us and affect our relationships with God and others.

Because we will center our lives around the things that offer us seenness.

Which is otherwise known as idolatry.

What's Your Fig Leaf?

We Christians can easily pinpoint idolatry in the world around us, but because we often wrap our idolatry in religious language and actions or choose idols that are "acceptable" to our fellow Christians, we have a much harder time seeing ourselves accurately and recognizing where we're malformed.

Sometimes we even fall into ongoing patterns of "using" God to be seen by others. This practice is exactly what Jesus addressed in Matthew 6:1: "Be careful not to practice your righteousness in front of others to be seen by them. Otherwise, you have no reward with your Father in heaven." He then lists ways we like to practice our religion for others to see—giving away our money, praying, and fasting—hoping they'll conclude we're holy (and we'll, therefore, get a shot of assurance, validation, and momentary applause).

In other words, as Christians, we aren't exempt from centering our lives around the things that offer us seenness in this world. We, too, have our fig-leaf strategies.

What is yours? Perhaps your strategy involves numbing out or zoning out, staying busy, avoiding conflict or difficult conversations, isolating yourself, seeking to do everything you do perfectly, exploding in anger or feeling overwhelmed, shutting down, peacefaking, involving yourself in religious or philanthropic activity, taking charge so you can stay in control, thinking through and planning for the worst possible scenario, analyzing and seeking information, helping others in the hopes that they'll help you, advocating for yourself or others, or seeking fun and lightheartedness in every conversation and situation.

Consider these questions to help you determine your fig leaf:

1. Are you a settled soul in relation to God and other people? If not, what is your unsettledness most consistently connected to, and what is your first line of defense to calm that unsettledness?

2. What do you do on a daily basis to outrun your unsettledness? In other words, what "turns the volume down" on your unsettledness?

3. Do you do anything to mask the unsettledness? To prove yourself or validate yourself in the eyes of God or others?

4. What reactions do you call upon when a person or circumstance cuts too close to your vulnerabilities or your wound of being unseen? For example, do you explode in anger, go numb, try to ignore your hurt, fawn, or fight?

Often, we can identify our fig-leaf strategies by looking for what we most heavily lean on in daily life when difficult circumstances arise and—here's the key—that become exacerbated over time. It's the button we're hitting over and over and over (and more and more often) to feel safe and settled. And it's the button we're hitting over and over and over to feel seen.

Now, a painfully difficult question: Does your strategy center on you or on God? In other words, is there any hint of idolatry involved?

In our daily lives we often, without even thinking about it, shove God out of the way. Why? Because our strategies for keeping unsettledness at bay are within our control and have generally worked for us for many years!

We wouldn't run the same play over and over in a football game unless it proved successful. But at some point, our strategies stop working because, although we've underemphasized the hidden parts of ourselves and tried to keep them tightly tucked away, those parts eventually begin to own us.

For example, as I got older, I became compulsive about achieving, accomplishing, and producing. The more I felt unsettled about my place in our church, the more I tried to get involved with or volunteer for in order to "turn down the volume" on the pain of feeling lost and overlooked. I was always seeking one more hit, one more moment of "success." The drive to perform was my proof of life: I do, therefore I exist. I do, therefore I am worth "seeing." Trouble was, the unsettledness and compulsivity were starting to own me; I could no longer hear the still, small voice of God whispering, "I love you. Just sit with me. It's okay to say no to that opportunity." I could no longer be still.

Whatever our strategy may be, the parts we're trying to quieten take on power, causing us to do what we don't want to do, for reasons we can't fully understand. Like Paul, we could say, "I do not do the good that I want to do, but I practice the evil that I do not want to do. Now if I do what I do not want, I am no longer the one that does it, but it is the sin that lives in me" (Rom. 7:19–20).

It's the sin that lives in me. Our strategies that originally set out to save us from pain become sin. Our responses to wounds from others become weapons with which we wound ourselves.

Our strategies keep us from meaningful connection with others. We hurt people with our strategies, just as we are hurt by theirs.

This is how we contribute to our own unseenness.

I can look back now and see how my fig-leaf strategy played out specifically in my friendships. For friendship to grow, it requires vulnerability, and vulnerability and performance cannot coexist. I wanted friendship without the risk of vulnerability; therefore, I struggled with friendship for many years. I spent so much energy shielding my insecurities and my true desires, needs, and preferences (as I'd learned to do) from the sight of others. I was more intent on impressing people with my success, ability, work, and performance than I was connecting with people through vulnerability. I was more intent on being seen and validated than I was on seeing others and loving them.

Flimsy Fig Leaves

However noble, externally successful, religious, spiritual, or culturally acceptable our strategies are, if they center our worth and seenness around something other than God, we're choosing a way of life based on the belief that God is a God who doesn't see. Period.

We are seeking safety and security in something other than the God Who Sees.

We're sewing our own fig leaves.

I look back over the course of my life and see my strategy of performing (and hiding) *everywhere*. I can see clear crossroads when someone's spoken expectation of me and God's leading in my life came into conflict, and I was faced with a choice. The choice was performing in the expected way to be seen by others—validated, accepted, approved—or obeying the God Who Sees. The choice was a dilemma because my obedience would cost me, making me feel like a disappointment to people I loved and wanted to approve of me. I felt my vulnerability showing and feared my fig leaf being exposed.

Paul's words in Galatians 1:10 describe the conundrum: "For am I now trying to persuade people, or God? Or am I striving to please people? If I were still trying to please people, I would not be a servant of Christ."

To be clear, the choice of obedience was not related to right or wrong. The obedience was about being me—the person God created and gifted me to be. Sometimes people want us and even expect us to be people we aren't, and if we chase their approval, we end up hiding our God-given gifts, skills, stories, and personality away, even eventually forgetting who we are.

Too many times, when I came to that crossroads of pleasing God or pleasing man, I chose to hide myself away in pursuit of being seen by others. I didn't trust God could hold me or sustain me through the disappointment of others. I didn't think I could withstand their disapproval or the increased pressure I knew would follow. I didn't really believe he was a God Who Sees and who, as he sees, protects, defends, helps, sustains, loves, and rejoices in me.

The God Who Sees never shames, guilts, manipulates, condemns, or expresses disappointment. He saw us long before we could disappoint him, long before we first saw him. In fact, he saw us even in the garden, when Adam and Eve were stitching together their fig leaves. He knew us when he promised the deceiving serpent, "I will put hostility between you and the woman, and between your offspring and her offspring. He will strike your head, and you will strike his heel" (Gen. 3:15). In other words, the serpent smugly claiming victory over God watched as his shining moment crumbled into defeat. Through the woman who sinned would come the Savior, Jesus Christ. And through him, a return to the garden where men and women didn't run and hide from God or one another.

To add heft to his promise, as a precursor and guarantee, God did some sewing of his own. He "made clothing from skins for the man and his wife, and he clothed them" (Gen. 3:21). An animal was killed—the first death recorded in Scripture—in order for Adam and Eve to be covered in the love and provision of God. Consider the contrast between a novice's flimsy sewn covering and the covering made with God's own hands.

We will spend much more time in future chapters exploring our seenness in Christ, but briefly consider the clothing God has clothed us with in Christ, the Lamb of God who died so we might live—we're clothed in his righteousness! Like Adam and Eve, he has given us a guarantee—the Holy Spirit—that one day soon we'll be further clothed with our heavenly body.

Our flimsy fig leaves look so silly, so prideful, and so impotent in comparison to the covering God has given us.

And this covering is not to hide us away; it is to invite us into the light of day to walk with him, unhindered in relationship with him and in freedom with others.

In your unseenness, in your vulnerable state, he sees you in this way. He is pleased with you. He delights in you. He's taken care of any obstacle or hindrance to your closeness with him—all so that you might enjoy him.

So, how do we become people with settled souls? We come out of hiding. We walk in the light of day, fully present and fully ourselves because we know we are fully loved by the God Who Sees. And we can release our silly, impotent strategies that we've wrongly believed would earn our seenness.

We cannot earn what we already have.

We don't have to be like Eve, trying to see like God.

We don't have to be like Sarai, attempting to be seen by God in our predetermined way.

And we don't need fig leaves because we're covered and clothed by Christ.

For Further Reflection

1. What is your strategy? How is it working for you? Are you getting any "hits" from it?

2. What is the vulnerable part of you this strategy attempts to cover?

3. Do you believe God sees you? What do you imagine is reflected in his eyes when he looks at you?

4. What would it mean for you to "come out of hiding"? What actions would that require? What risk would you have to accept?

5. What do you need to repent of regarding your pursuit of seenness by others?

Chapter 5

HIDING FROM OBEDIENCE

G od appeared to Hagar in her most vulnerable state and
asked questions meant to locate her in relation to him:
Where have you come from? And *where are you going?* Although
she replied matter-of-factly, "I'm running away from my mistress
Sarai" (Gen. 16:8), we've experienced the moment between them
as pregnant with pain and distress.

As we previously discovered, God's response is surprising and
perhaps alarming: "Go back to your mistress and submit to her
authority" (v. 9). Wouldn't we rather see him comfort her, ask
clarifying questions to draw out her every thought and emotion,
or perhaps even announce his alignment with Hagar against Sarai?

It was his kindness, however, that led him to instruct her to
get on her feet and return home.

She was not meant to stay in the desert. She was meant to
return because to return was to place herself once again under
the covenant God had made with Abram. God had promised to
prosper him and make his family into a great nation that would,

in turn, bless the entire world. God's instruction to return and submit to Sarai was a call to return and submit to the promises and provision of God.

Following his command, as if in pointed emphasis (and before Hagar uttered a word), God launched into the proclamation of a promise specific to her that echoed his first promise to Abram: he would give her a legacy through children and grandchildren and great-grandchildren beyond number. The legacy's foundation would be the child in Hagar's womb: Ishmael, meaning "God hears."

In these words, God offered Hagar a hope and a future. In these promises, he offered her his compassion and mercy.

But for Hagar to receive these promises and provision—to live in the light of day—would mean returning to live beside Sarai as she *also* received these promises and provision. God would later describe himself to Moses as "a compassionate and gracious God, slow to anger and abounding in faithful love and truth, maintaining faithful love to a thousand generations, forgiving iniquity, rebellion, and sin" (Exod. 34:6–7). Could Hagar watch God be generously compassionate and merciful to the one who had inflicted on her such pain? Who was herself a sinner and had dismissed and disregarded Hagar? Who had treated her with such harshness?

The better question is, can we?

Anger's Attractive Promises

When my eyes opened to stark reality and I felt the pain of how others had wounded me, I felt such heavy grief and sadness that it took every ounce of energy to carry it through each day.

But the sadness, as I previously mentioned, quickly turned to anger.

I felt acutely angry when I felt the weight of the consequences of others' sin falling on me to bear. It seemed unfair that I was forced to enter an arena of struggle and pain and fighting for forgiveness. I felt like a fool for dutifully standing in the shadows as a pastor's wife and incessantly trying to make my husband look good, for overlooking offenses and yellow flags along the way, and for believing the best in others. What was even true anymore? What was right and good?

Kyle was fighting in a different arena of struggle and pain— one of crushing discipline from the Lord, one of cavernous exploration of his heart and how his idolatrous desire for respect and admiration had led him to overlook and dismiss me, and I praise God for his true repentance and godly sorrow.

But I was still so angry. We were fighting together for a better day, but most of the time I was just fighting him in all my frustration, fury, and disillusionment. And because the friend who had hurt me was unwilling to have a conversation based in reality—I certainly tried—I had conversation after conversation in my head with her, fighting to convince her of my perspective and my feelings.

I make no apologies for my anger. Righteous anger is a proper response to sin. Righteous anger tells us something is not right and invites us to seek change in order to make things right.

Almost immediately, however, the righteous anger soured into self-righteous anger; and, boy, does self-righteous anger feel good to the flesh. The notion of being "right" can easily become a point of pride and a weapon wielded to punish. That notion invites us to complain, give up, retaliate, spread gossip, overlook the speck in our own eye, and excuse ourselves from the direct commands of God to be kind, tenderhearted, patient, and merciful.

I'd never felt such a wave of anger like this one.

I knew how to respond to my own sin: confess, repent, and kill that creeping vine I'd feverishly watered. The gospel I'd heard preached my entire life, over and over, spoke a liturgy over me: the body of Christ, broken for you; the blood of Christ, poured out for you.

But I didn't know what to do when the sins of others came so close and cut so deep. I knew forgiveness was the command in play, just as returning was the command for Hagar, but I'll be frank: I didn't want to think of the body of Christ, broken for *her*, the blood of Christ, poured out for *her*.

I wanted instead to stew in my anger, rehearse the reasons I had a right to it, and tell God what I thought he ought to do as a result. I could not fathom forgiving, for I had yet to drink to the dregs every last reason I could find to be angry.

In other words, I kept getting stuck. I wanted to forgive, but then I remembered what specifically I needed to forgive, and I'd end up right back in my own fury.

This point—sitting in the desert with the offered promises and provision in one hand and the tandem difficult command of obedience in the other—is the point in the progression of our stories of unseenness where many of us get stuck, sometimes for a lifetime.

Notice the progression of where we've walked together so far in this book: we've acknowledged the various categories of unseenness, we've specifically named the pain of unseenness, and we've explored the ways we attempt to cover the resulting shame and insecurity with fig-leaf strategies.

There is good and healthy movement about this progression: we're getting somewhere with God. He has received us in our lament and confession, and he's moving us toward healing. However, now we've reached the part of the progression where he's pointing toward the pathway before us labeled "forgiveness"—a releasing of others from the debt they owe us for neglecting or refusing to see us. It's not as if, the moment we set our face toward home, that we must immediately put the pain of the past behind us—as if we can control it or we're doing something wrong if we can't. He's simply asking us to get on our feet and begin walking the path he's prescribed.

As we see the path coming into view, just as we respond in our flesh when we hear God tell Hagar, "Return," we hesitate. God has been mercifully gentle with us so far, reminding us over and over that he sees and is for us and placing his healing balm on our wound. The path he's now asking us to start down feels as if he's taking the other person's side and asking us to do the same, pressing us toward something we don't want to do. And even when we want to do the right thing, we feel incapable of doing it.

As God offered Hagar promises of the good that waited for her, his Word promises his prescribed path is one of life and joy: "Blessed are the merciful, for they will be shown mercy" (Matt. 5:7). It's difficult to believe blessing comes to us as we are merciful to others. The opposite appears true, for anger makes attractive promises of its own.

Clearly, we have a choice. We can trust him and move forward, accepting his invitation toward the path of life.

Or we can trust ourselves and what seems right to us, hiding ourselves from obedience.

The wounded can so easily become the wounder.

When You Can't Stand God's Mercy

When I think of hiding from obedience, I think of Jonah. Jonah was tasked by God to go to Nineveh with a message. Specifically, God said to him, "Get up! Go to the great city of Nineveh and preach against it because their evil has come up before me" (Jonah 1:2). In essence, God called Jonah to head into enemy territory—Nineveh was the capital of Assyria, a nation who had brutally destroyed Jonah's people—with a difficult and confrontational message, sure to be ignored and derided.

In Jonah's mind, only danger awaited him in obedience. So, although he did get up, instead of setting off to Nineveh, he ran in the exact opposite direction and hopped on a boat headed even farther from his home, all in an attempt to flee the Lord's presence and the Lord's calling.

The Lord, ever-present and all-seeing, met Jonah and the ship with a terrible storm, an unsubtle invitation and merciful second chance for obedience that Jonah again refused. Believing in pagan gods, the sailors onboard cast lots to discover whose actions caused the storm. The lot fell on Jonah, who at the time was asleep in the ship's hold. After much discussion and at Jonah's request, the sailors hurled Jonah into the sea to stop the storm.

As he sank to the bottom of the ocean, he thought perhaps he'd finally outrun the sight of the Lord, saying, "When you threw me into the depths, into the heart of the seas, the current overcame me. All your breakers and your billows swept over me. And I said,

'I have been banished from your sight'" (2:3–4). However, instead of smugness at this realization, he caught a glimpse of what truly being separated from God's presence would result in—a grave-yard in the sea. Knowingly and resolutely, he cried out, "Salvation belongs to the LORD" (2:9).

And he was saved.

God, "a compassionate and gracious God, slow to anger and abounding in faithful love and truth, maintaining faithful love to a thousand generations, forgiving iniquity, rebellion, and sin" (Exod. 34:6–7), once again extended mercy toward Jonah by appointing a fish to swallow him and keep him alive.

After three days and nights, the fish spit Jonah out, and Jonah went straight to Nineveh in obedience to the Lord—finally. "Jonah set out on the first day of his walk in the city and pro-claimed, 'In forty days Nineveh will be demolished!'" (Jonah 3:4).

The shortest sermon ever preached! And amazingly, it was the most effective sermon ever preached, for "the people of Nineveh believed God. They proclaimed a fast and dressed in sackcloth—from the greatest of them to the least" (v. 5).

The entire city believed and repented. The king issued a proc-lamation and had it published throughout the city: "Everyone must call out earnestly to God. Each must turn from his evil ways and from his wrongdoing. Who knows? God may turn and relent; he may turn from his burning anger so that we will not perish" (3:8–9).

In fact, that's exactly what happened. God, "a compassionate and gracious God, slow to anger and abounding in faithful love and truth, maintaining faithful love to a thousand generations, forgiving iniquity, rebellion, and sin," "saw their actions—that they had turned from their evil ways—so God relented from the disaster he had threatened them with. And he did not do it" (3:10).

How would you feel if you saw this type of response to a call for repentance from a people as evil and brutal as those from Sodom and Gomorrah? And what if you were the one to preach that sermon? I'd be humbled and amazed, especially after being so reluctant to go in the first place.

But Jonah was not amazed, nor was he humbled. Instead, "Jonah was greatly displeased and became furious" (4:1). Why? He pointed his accusing finger at God and said, "That's why I fled toward Tarshish in the first place. I knew that you are a gracious and compassionate God, slow to anger, abounding in faithful love, and one who relents from sending disaster" (4:2). He subsequently asked God to take his life because he didn't want to see the people of Nineveh—violent pagans—receive God's mercy.

In other words, Jonah saw the path of life coming into view and didn't just hesitate. He stopped in his tracks, folded his arms, and refused to budge *because Jonah knew God would forgive the people he didn't like.*

His anger felt better to him.

So he retreated outside the city, built himself a nice little shelter, and sat down to watch what would become of this people he despised. Perhaps he longed for Nineveh and all its people to burn after all. Perhaps he recounted in his mind all the wrongs Nineveh had done against his people, stoking his anger. Perhaps he soaked in bitterness and cynicism.

Yet even as Jonah stewed in his self-righteous anger, God continued extending his invitation to Jonah to walk the pathway paved with mercy, grace, and life. God appointed a plant to grow as shade for Jonah. *Here, Jonah, have a touch of relief from the heat.* Still, Jonah wouldn't budge.

The book of Jonah ends here, without resolution. We gather that God saved Nineveh from destruction, and we're left to wonder what became of Jonah.

We do know that Jonah took refuge in his shelter built upon a foundation of his anger, his reluctant obedience souring into bitterness. Because he wouldn't walk the path of obedience with God, he missed out on his own joy and the joy of seeing life transformation in himself and others. *He missed out on God.*

The summary of Jonah's life is that he knew God would be compassionate toward his enemies, and he couldn't stand to watch it unfold. He'd rather have been proven right. He'd rather have seen people experience the wrath of God. He'd rather have died himself.

When Anger Sours into Bitterness

The same things happen to us when we hide from obedience: our hearts turn hard. We'd rather be proven right than see God's mercy and grace transform repentant souls, and we take refuge in a shelter built with anger.

The result is a life characterized by bitterness. There can never be resolution or peace regarding our wound of unseenness because we must keep our anger alive. We can't walk out of the desert and into the promises and provision of God because we can't stand to watch God pour his mercy out on those who've hurt us.

I've seen this play out in my own life, specifically in relation to the friend who had wounded me.

When I look back at my journals from around this time, I read words of comparison, replaying hurts, self-pity, frustration with her, and finding faults in her.

I was Jonah, sitting in my refuge of anger, festering in bitterness. And that bitterness was starting to spill over into my words and actions. I was irritable, unforgiving, and desiring for God to be merciful to me but not to her.

When I realized the precarious place I was in, I was terrified. I immediately thought of Hebrews 12:15: "Make sure that no one falls short of the grace of God and that no root of bitterness springs up, causing trouble and defiling many."

The snare of bitterness is dangerous—not just for the one caught in it but for everyone else around her. Our unchecked bitterness is characterized as a weed that springs out of the ground in a beautiful, thriving garden that eventually takes root and then takes over, choking out life and vitality and ruining the garden. And although we think we can mask it, unchecked bitterness doesn't stay hidden in the heart. Rather, it chokes out the life and joy not only in ourselves but also in the people around us.

The internal creeping vine becomes external.

This is why, as God brings the pathway of forgiveness into view, it is good and right for us to take his hand and let him lead us there. If we don't, our anger will become self-righteous, stagnating and atrophying into bitterness.

But if you're anything like me, bitterness has already crept in. How can we begin to address and root out what is threatening to destroy us?

Defining Bitterness

In his book *Overcoming Bitterness*, Stephen Viars describes three components to bitterness, all of which are observable from my example above:

> *Bitter conditions:* difficult or painful circumstances we face in life, including unseenness

> *Internal bitterness:* replaying hurts and disappointments in our minds, which develops into antagonism, hostility, or resentfulness

> *External actions:* the words, actions, and choices that result when we act upon our internal bitterness[1]

Notably, Scripture tells us that difficult circumstances or bitter conditions don't automatically lead to internal and external bitterness but rather can be the catalyst for our growth in faith, endurance, hope, and joy.

So there must be something specific that poisons our hearts, turning difficult circumstances into bitterness. What is it?

In the *English Standard Version*, the author of Hebrews places quotation marks around "root of bitterness" in Hebrews 12:15. The writer is referencing the time when Moses renewed the covenant between God and his people as they prepared to enter the promised land. He said, "Beware lest there be among you *a root bearing poisonous and bitter fruit*, one who, when he hears the

---

1. Stephen Viars, *Overcoming Bitterness* (Grand Rapids, MI: Baker Books, 2021).

words of this sworn covenant, blesses himself in his heart, saying, 'I shall be safe, though I walk in the stubbornness of my heart.' This will lead to the sweeping away of moist and dry alike" (Deut. 29:18–19 ESV, emphasis added).

In *The Message*, Eugene Peterson describes this stubborn person as one "who hears the words of the Covenant-oath but exempts himself, thinking, 'I'll live just the way I please, thank you,' and ends up ruining life for everybody" (Deut. 29:18–19).

In other words, difficult circumstances turn into bitterness when we begin exempting ourselves, telling ourselves we are the exceptions to the ways and commands of God.

Suffering? Why would God allow me to experience such suffering and hardship? Look at all I've done for him!

Forgive and pray for my enemies? But look at what I am having to endure with this person in my life!

Notice my own exceptional thinking I described at the beginning of this chapter as I felt God's gentle invitation toward the pathway of forgiveness: *But I'd never felt such a wave of anger like this one.* Almost as if I was entitled to my bitterness.

Righteous anger becomes self-righteous anger in that moment. An honest acknowledgment and declaration to God about the pain of sin is agreeing with him about it—this is righteous anger. Setting ourselves in God's position as a result, seeking vindication or vengeance, believing anger is our right? That is self-righteous anger that bears destructive fruit, the first of which is bitterness.

Internal bitterness then becomes like a phone notification, constantly going off: *Remember what that person said or did? Rehearse it. Cherish it. Recall it. Drink that bitter cup down again and again.*

The more we give attention to the notifications, the more we balk at God's ways and commands, and the more they appear to be death to us rather than life. Our internal bitterness tells us we will be more blessed in our shelter of anger than to forgive and that we have a right to lash out, disengage, or isolate. It says we have a right to harden our hearts.

This is how bitterness defiles many but first defiles us.

Get Out Your Gardening Tools

What do we do when we recognize bitterness in our response to feeling unseen?

First, we confess and repent. God has given us these beautiful and always accessible gifts to clear our blurry eyes, refresh our hope, and make soft our hardened hearts.

Second, we must look at the root of our bitterness, not just the rotten fruit. We may think anger is the root, but anger is a secondary emotion. What lies beneath anger is hurt and fear.

As we've already established, we must name how we feel about our wound of unseenness to God and let him speak his balm of truth to us, but this highlights the need to do so *repeatedly* until God has worked his healing into every crevice and detail of the hurt.

While unrestrained anger is sinful, if we believe all anger is always wrong and to be avoided at all costs, instead of letting our anger signal an unhealed hurt, we attempt to suppress it and move on. Suppressing never works in the end and is, in fact, detrimental.

So, if you're to look at the root and not just the fruit of bitterness, you must ask, "What unacknowledged hurt do I have?" And it might also be clarifying to ask yourself, "How am I suppressing the hurt?" And, "Why am I suppressing the hurt?"

As we "put off" unhelpful and even sinful responses to hurt through confession, repentance, and digging out the roots—"Let all bitterness, anger and wrath, shouting and slander be removed from you, along with all malice" (Eph. 4:31)—God then helps us "put on" helpful and right responses: "Be kind and compassionate to one another, forgiving one another, just as God also forgave you in Christ" (v. 32).

The "putting on" is an imitation of God and how he's loved us, and it's a putting on of Christ, acting as he has acted toward us.

I love gardening, so when I think of this putting off and putting on process, I think of a healthy, vibrant garden. Vigilant weeding is necessary to keep bitterness from taking root in our hearts. But the garden also needs water and sunlight for the fruitful, beautiful plants to grow.

It's interesting to me, then, that Jesus is called the light of the world[2] and our living water.[3] Our hearts need constant access to him, constant "intake" of him if we're to stay healthy. We must, as the writer of Hebrews says, "consider him" (12:3). How does considering him hinder bitterness from taking root when we encounter pain?

When we look upon Jesus as he's described in Hebrews 12, we find one who not only experienced pain from others but who also willingly absorbed the consequences for them and provided a way for their forgiveness: "Therefore, since we also have such a large cloud of witnesses surrounding us, let us lay aside every

---

2. John 8:12.
3. John 7:37–39.

hindrance and the sin that so easily ensnares us. Let us run with endurance the race that lies before us, keeping our eyes on Jesus, the pioneer and perfecter of our faith. For the joy that lay before him, he endured the cross, despising the shame, and sat down at the right hand of the throne of God" (vv. 1–3).

Faithful brothers and sisters who have endured in the faith call to us from the pathway of forgiveness ahead. (Notably, they see us!) The race set before us leads through this path, but bitterness stops us in our tracks; it keeps us from making progress in the Christian life.

We're told to keep our eyes on Jesus. What do we find when we look at him? We see he himself endured bitter conditions: humiliation, hostility, and death. We see true injustice, true unseenness.

What does looking at him in light of our own bitter conditions do? We can walk forward—even run forward—without getting sidetracked because the One who invites us down the pathway of forgiveness has done exactly what he's asking us to do. In fact, he's done more: "In struggling against sin, you have not yet resisted to the point of shedding your blood" (v. 4).

In our own pain and bitterness, we can easily dwell on how we've been misunderstood, overlooked, disregarded, and unjustly treated. Jesus, however, is the one who knows true injustice, having endured far more than we ever will and yet doing so without sin. He did it willingly, for you and for me, yet he is patient and compassionate with us, ready to receive us and help us in our own bitter conditions.

We're called to "consider him," but, notably, in this passage Jesus has considered something as well. He's considered, or looked, at what was to come after his suffering: the joy that awaited him, knowing he'd provided us salvation and pleased his Father.

When we look beyond our own bitter conditions and imagine the end of the pathway ahead, we see there can be joy for us, too. The joy of being free of poisonous anger. The joy of knowing God is pleased with our faith and obedience. And the joy of hearing, "Well done, good and faithful servant!" (Matt. 25:21).

When Your Stomach Rumbles, Consider This

At the end of Hebrews 12, the author connects his instructions regarding bitterness to a specific person: "Make sure that no one falls short of the grace of God and that no root of bitterness springs up, causing trouble and defiling many. And make sure that there isn't any immoral or irreverent person like Esau, who sold his birthright in exchange for a single meal. For you know that later, when he wanted to inherit the blessing, he was rejected, even though he sought it with tears, because he didn't find any opportunity for repentance" (vv. 15–17).

The person connected to bitterness is Esau, the twin brother of Jacob and the firstborn of the two. As the firstborn, Esau was the inheriting brother; all the riches of his father belonged to him. However, Esau came in from hunting one day, starving. His brother Jacob had a steaming bowl of stew ready, and Esau wanted a bowl right then. Jacob offered a trade: the birthright for a bowl of stew. It seems a ridiculous and outbalanced trade, but Esau agreed. In the exchange of a bowl for the birthright, Jacob became the inheriting child instead of Esau.

Why does the writer of Hebrews reference this story in relation to bitterness? Because Esau's story is about immediate gratification and misplaced desire. As Stephen Viars says, "Sinful bitterness always begins with misplaced desires."[4]

As we come along in the progression to the pathway of forgiveness, we can understand Jonah. We know God will be gracious and merciful not just to us but also to our repentant enemies. Can we stand to watch that story unfold, or should we get up and run in the opposite direction?

We can also understand Esau. We want vindication, and we want it right now—immediate gratification. We want that person to get what she deserves, and we want it right now. We want that person to apologize before we will take a step toward forgiveness, and we want that apology right now.

But we have Jesus!

We are inheriting children, yet we want the bowl of stew that we may stew in it.

So, when your stomach rumbles with anger, when you want what you want right now, consider him. Consider your forever birthright. Consider the riches of Christ: his indwelling presence, forgiveness, and steadfast love. Consider the removal of condemnation and influx of favor and a place in his eternal kingdom. Consider what Christ did to earn you that birthright. And consider how quickly the stew will vanish and how unsatisfied you'll soon be.

Bitterness cannot take root as you consider these things.

And the pathway of forgiveness begins to look like the pathway to life, indeed.

Hagar returned to her life.

So can we.

---

4. Viars, *Overcoming Bitterness*, 86.

For Further Reflection

1. What step of obedience is God calling you to take in order to exit the desert of unseenness?

2. Is self-righteous anger or bitterness hindering you from obedience?

3. How has exceptional thinking contributed to whatever bitterness or unforgiveness is in your heart?

4. How does looking at Jesus, as in Hebrews 12, give you perspective on obedience and bitterness?

5. In what way are you exchanging your birthright for an immediate bowl of stew? How will you practically forego immediacy and trust Jesus to care for you?

Part Three

HIDDEN

Chapter 6

HIDDEN IN CHRIST

H agar returned.

She went home, folding herself into Abram's family and God's promise. We have no record of her return travels or the response of Sarai or Abram when she arrived back at their doorstep. We can certainly imagine the courage it took to show her face again, belly swelling with the child whose conception had tangled their home life and their future. The only peek we're given into Hagar's return is found in Genesis 16:15–16: "So Hagar gave birth to Abram's son, and Abram named his son (whom Hagar bore) Ishmael. Abram was eighty-six years old when Hagar bore Ishmael to him."

And so, life continued. When Ishmael was thirteen, God appeared to Abram and changed his name to Abraham, meaning "father of a multitude," although he was only a father to one and reaching the centenarian mark. Each time God appeared to Abraham and with each word he spoke, the promise of a child born to Sarah (God changed her name, too) came more and more into view. God repeated the promise, nuanced the promise, colored in the promise, emphasized the promise.

A child was still to come: the true firstborn.

As much as God cared and provided for Hagar and Ishmael, Ishmael could never be the child of promise. Man cannot create or control the supernatural. And man cannot thwart the plans and promises of God, no matter how much of a tangle they make.

All along, God's plan was Isaac. And the plan would be enacted by faith, not flesh.

And then, suddenly, after all those years of waiting and despairing and cutting her own path, God's plan came to fruition: "The LORD came to Sarah as he had said, and the LORD did for Sarah what he had promised. Sarah became pregnant and bore a son to Abraham in his old age, at the appointed time God had told him" (Gen. 21:1–2).

Isaac's birth complicated Abraham's home life even more than Ishmael's birth: "The child grew and was weaned, and Abraham held a great feast on the day Isaac was weaned. But Sarah saw the son mocking—the one Hagar the Egyptian had borne to Abraham. So she said to Abraham, 'Drive out this slave with her son, for the son of this slave will not be a coheir with my son Isaac!' This was very distressing to Abraham because of his son" (Gen. 21:8–11).

The child of flesh mocked and persecuted the child of promise, and God responded by telling Abraham, "Do not be distressed about the boy and about your slave. Whatever Sarah says to you, listen to her, because your offspring will be traced through Isaac, and I will also make a nation of the slave's son because he is your offspring" (21:12–13).

For a second time, Hagar wandered in the desert. For a second time, she despaired for her life and the life of her son. For a second time, God heard her weeping and visited her in the wilderness. For a second time, God saw her need and provided for her—this time a well from which to drink. And, for a second time, God kept his promise to bless Abram's offspring: "God was with the boy, and he grew; he settled in the wilderness and became an archer" (21:20).

God was with the boy. He watched over him, provided for him, and made a way for him.

But this time, Hagar was not instructed by God to return home.

The Promised Child Endangered

What are we to make of this? We've walked so closely with Hagar in these pages that this feels like a sad and abrupt parting.

Hagar's story has so far given us permission to acknowledge how we've experienced unseenness and how it's impacted us. She's taught us that trusting and obeying God sets our feet on the path of life. The inclusion of Hagar's story in Scripture has been a balm to our souls, comforting us with the news that God sees the least of these and hears our cries of affliction.

And she has led us back to Sarah.

Sarah is no saint. Her story so far has exposed our own sinful strategies for seeking visibility and resolution to our restlessness by taking matters into our own hands.

Is there any hope for these two rivals?

Is there any hope for us in the mess and hurt of our unseenness? A new fig-leaf strategy isn't our hope. Holding anger and unforgiveness toward others isn't our hope. Blaming ourselves or others isn't our hope. Our unseenness has been a wound we ourselves can't heal or overcome; we've certainly tried.

But Hagar has led us back to Sarah.

There is something here for us to see, for Sarah has birthed the child of promise.

According to Galatians 4:22–23, Hagar's child, forged by the flesh, can only bear children into slavery to this flesh. In other words, she represents futile attempts at self-righteousness and self-correction. Sarah's child, forged by God himself, bears children into freedom from this flesh. She represents the freedom that can only come through faith. Hagar is not the villain, nor is Sarah the hero of the story. A God who keeps his promises is the hero, and Scripture tells us to trace our need for hope and restoration not through Hagar's lineage but rather through Sarah's. We can entrust Hagar and Ishmael to God and follow Sarah to freedom.

What freedom is this?

The Lord Will See to It

After Isaac's birth, God once again appeared to Abraham, not with a promise but rather with a test. He required Abraham to go on a three-day journey to Mount Moriah to offer Isaac there as a burnt offering. For any parent, this would have been true terror to hear, but Abraham immediately obeyed.

The story of God commanding Abraham to offer Isaac as a sacrifice can be confusing and terrifying, but as D. A. Carson points out, "In the pagan religions of the time, it was not all that uncommon for parents to sacrifice their own sons. It was a mark of devotion. But the whole point of this account is that this is not what God wants. How can you possibly please God, the God of the Bible, by destroying your children?"[1]

Perhaps as Abraham gathered his son and the tools of death and began his journey, he thought back to the moment many years before when God had first appeared to him and made a covenant with him. The Lord had in that moment promised him a child, a child from his own body who would later produce a great nation and possess an abundant land. Abraham had believed the Lord could and would do this for him—a belief that God had credited to him as righteousness. Abraham had then asked for some sort of confirmation, and God had requested he gather several animals for sacrifice. As was customary when making covenants in his day, Abraham cut the animals in half—a visible demonstration from the weaker party of what would happen if he broke the covenant—and would then offer his oath of loyalty to God and his promise of obedience to the covenant by walking between the divided animals.[2]

In those three days with Isaac, as he anticipated what was to come, could it be that Abraham considered in detail how he'd broken his covenant with God? He'd lied to foreign leaders, identifying Sarah as his sister, leaving her unprotected. He'd agreed to Sarah's foolish plan to get the promised child through Hagar. He'd turned a blind eye to Sarah's harsh treatment of Hagar. He was a sinner, sin required justice, and that justice for sin required sacrifice.

1. D. A. Carson, *The God Who Is There* (Grand Rapids, MI: Baker Books, 2010), 53.
2. Genesis 15.

There would be blood, a payment for breaking covenant. And how precious the sacrifice now being called for! His firstborn from Sarah, the child of promise.

Perhaps in his agony, Abraham was also puzzled. How could the God requiring justice for sin also be the God of promise? God had promised this boy would kick-start a world of blessing. Was he going back on his word? How could both justice and promise of blessing come together?

Breaking into his father's thoughts as they walked together, Isaac said, "'The fire and the wood are here, but where is the lamb for the burnt offering?' Abraham answered, 'God himself will provide the lamb for the burnt offering, my son.' Then the two of them walked on together" (Gen. 22:7–8).

Isaac knew the sacrifice couldn't be completed without an animal. Abraham didn't know how the debt of sin was going to be paid without crushing the promise, but he believed God would provide the sacrifice.

He had reason to believe. Previously, when God appeared to make a covenant with Abraham and he'd gathered the requested animals for sacrifice and divided them in two, just as he'd prepared to walk between them to commit his obedience to the covenant, Abraham fell into a deep sleep and "suddenly great terror and darkness descended on him" (Gen. 15:12). God himself, in the form of a smoking firepot and a flaming torch, passed between the divided animals, confirming the covenant. "Who by his actions announced, 'May what has happened to these animals happen to me if I fail to keep my oath?' Not the weaker party. Rather, the Lord of the cosmos traversed the bloody alley to announce to Abraham and his offspring that he would not fail."[3]

In other words, what God required, God would do. The promise did not depend on Abraham, on Sarah, on Hagar, on Ishmael, or even on Isaac. The promise depended on God's keeping of it.

And he did. Just as Abraham prepared to offer Isaac to God, God stopped him, and Abraham "looked up and saw a ram caught in the thicket by its horns. So Abraham went and took the ram and offered it as a burnt offering in place of his son. And Abraham named that place The LORD Will Provide" (Gen. 22:13–14).

"The Lord Will Provide"—literally "the Lord will *see to it.*" Stop and take that in. The name implies both a seeing of what is needed and a providing of that very thing. The God Who Sees has "seen to" provide what was needed and required. Justice and promise as one—in One. In Levitical sacrifice, the offerer provided the sacrifice, but Abraham said that God saw to it—he provided the sacrifice. He made it a matter of his responsibility.

God's seeing of sin and the resulting need for justice regarding that sin prompted his action. God's seeing of his promises also prompted his action. He provided all that was required and all that was needed.

The Son Not Spared

The ram died that day, and a son didn't. There was a penalty and a punishment for sin meted out on the sacrifice provided by

---

3. Sandra Richter, *The Epic of Eden* (Westmont, IL: IVP Academic, 2010), loc. 1211.

God. As a result, a father and a son walked down the mountain together, rejoicing in the God who "sees to it" to fulfill both his holy requirements and his promise.

The son who was spared, this son of promise, eventually fathered children and grandchildren and great-grandchildren—so many that they became a great nation. Over the course of hundreds of years, this nation went into Egypt during famine, became slaves, and then came out of Egypt, led by Moses, as free people. Led by Joshua, they fought for the land God promised them, and eventually, through David, established a city on *the very spot* Abraham and Isaac experienced God's provision of the ram. That city was Jerusalem, with its temple built on the mountain called The Lord Will Provide.

Years later in Jerusalem, another Father would put wood on the back of his Son and walk him up the hill. This Son is where Sarah and her child of promise point. Just as with Abraham, an offering for sin was required, not the sin of the Father or the Son but the sins of all humankind. But this time, on the mountain called The Lord Will Provide, there wasn't a ram in the thicket to substitute for the Son. Instead, the Son was the substitute for me and for you. The Son willingly laid his life down as the sacrifice. "Look, the Lamb of God, who takes away the sin of the world!"[4]

Why would he do this?

The apostle Paul brings his amazement at this sacrifice into a joy-filled monologue about the extent of God's love for us: "What, then, are we to say about these things? If God is for us, who is against us? He did not even spare his own Son but gave him up for us all. How will he not also with him *grant us everything*? Who can

---

4. John 1:29.

bring an accusation against God's elect? God is the one who justi-fies. Who is the one who condemns? Christ Jesus is the one who died, but even more, has been raised" (Rom. 8:31–34, emphasis added).

Because of his love for us, God has "seen to it." Before we could see our need, he knew us. While we were still under sin and its curse, he had already "seen to it" to provide the sacrifice for our sins so we could go down the mountain with our Father and live, amazed and rejoicing at what we were and are spared. We are spared condemnation and judgment. We are spared life and eternity apart from God. We are spared remaining in the disgusting filth of our sins. We are spared a lack of justice and vindication for sin committed against us. We are spared slavery to the flesh. And we are spared from needing fig leaves.

Justice and promise as one—in One.

The punishment has been taken. The promise of freedom has come to fruition.[5]

How great the love and justice of God! What God said to Abraham after he was tested, we can now say to God: "For now I know that you [love me], since you have not withheld your only son from me" (Gen. 22:12).

Seen, Yet Hidden

Colossians 3:3 tells us that we're both seen and hidden: "For you died, and your life is hidden with Christ in God."

Do you find it interesting that the God who sees would also call us hidden and count it as a positive thing?

---

5. Galatians 3:14.

This is a good time to stop and consider a definition of seenness.

So far in this book, we've specifically named types of unseenness and explored how we've felt in our unseenness. But have you considered its opposite? Have you, in your unseenness, stopped to consider what it would mean to you to be seen or feel seen? What would need to happen for you to know you are seen? How would you definitively know that God has seen you or others have seen you? What is the definition of seenness?

Many years ago, I led a group from our church on a mission trip to serve and support one of our partner ministries in Ethiopia. Our team met early one morning while it was still dark to begin our travels, and my husband and young boys dropped me off at the meeting spot. As they drove away, one of my sons rolled down the window and yelled out in an eerily spooky voice, "God is watching you!" It was if he was saying, "You guys better do a good job or else!" The team turned to me with wide eyes, unsure of how to digest his declaration, and then we all busted out laughing.

In his youth and limited vocabulary, what he was trying to convey, I think, wasn't, "God has his eye on you and is evaluating you, so you better do a good job," but rather, "God is watching over you. He is with you. And because he's with you, go serve together in peace and joy."

This is our God. He isn't nebulous or general; he is specific, near, personal, and engaged. For him to "see" us is not simply to take in the events of our lives with his eyes. To "see" in the biblical sense means he enters into the experience of our lives with us, is fully present with us in it, and knows us at the deepest level possible. He is not watching from afar; he is with us in it.

I experience being seen in friendship when I am at my most vulnerable with that person. I share something that feels raw, emotional, or difficult; and my friend responds in a way that lets me know I've been understood. Perhaps they reflect to me what they're hearing me say, or they give words to my emotions I haven't been able to find. Perhaps they speak a word of encouragement that soothes my despairing heart, or they serve me in a way that's meaningful to me. True seenness involves a deep, personal knowing within a deep, personal relationship. It considers the unique individuals involved: their personalities, experiences, desires, and abilities. And true seenness involves a loving response: tears to match my own, a hug, physical help, gentle correction, or kind words of hope.

This is precisely how Hagar knew she'd been seen by God: he personally attended to her at her most vulnerable, entered into her experience, acknowledged her feelings, and helped her navigate her situation. In addition, in a very profound way, she experienced his character and nature, specifically his omniscience and compassion.

We can know that we, too, are seen by God in this way by looking at the sacrifice of Christ on the cross and by looking at the resurrection of Christ in the empty tomb.

When we look at the cross, we find that God knew us before we knew ourselves. He saw our greatest need—reconciliation with God—and lovingly met this need, "making peace through his blood, shed on the cross" (Col. 1:20). Christ brought us back into an intimate relationship with God the Father. We can now know and be known without the separation sin and our fig-leaf strategies bring.

When we look at the empty tomb, we find an abundance of grace by which we live our lives for him and with him: "If by the one man's trespass, death reigned through that one man, *how much more* will those who receive the overflow of grace and the gift of righteousness reign in life through the one man, Jesus Christ" (Rom. 5:17, emphasis added). Or put another way, how will he not also through him grant us everything?

We were buried with Christ in his death, we are raised with Christ in his resurrection, and we currently live united with Christ. We know and are known with the deepest intimacy and affection. This is the seenness we long for, isn't it? And this—being "in Christ"—is what it means to be hidden in him. All that he has is ours.

Let us not miss, then, that "seeing" is the nature of God! And let us not miss that, in his seeing, he always acts. And let us not miss that when he acts, it is always good: a rescuing, delivering, providing, saving, and justice-wielding kind of good. His love is like that love of the friend who listens, leans in, accepts, and offers the best of herself in return, except he does it perfectly, is steadfastly available to us, and meets us with an all-knowing understanding. He engages us without tiring, without discomfort or distancing, without growing exasperated, and without condemnation.

There is a welcoming, a belonging, an acceptance that God gives us in Christ.

This is the freedom promised in Sarah's story: unhindered relationship with God. This freedom comes to us, not through our papered-together fig leaves or making ourselves worthy to be seen and validated but through faith in the child of promise—Christ himself.

Refuged

The Bible gives us a word picture to help us wrap our minds around the extent of God's "seeing" of us and acting for us: he is called our Refuge. Some of my favorite verses related to God being our Refuge are Psalm 5:11–12: "But let all who take refuge in you rejoice; let them shout for joy forever. May you shelter them, and may those who love your name boast about you. For you, Lord, bless the righteous one; you surround him with favor like a shield."

God isn't simply a fortress we can run and hide behind when the going gets tough; we are literally refuged or hidden in him at all times.

When I think of refuge, I think of the need for safety. The word immediately evokes for me a contrast between being in danger, assailed at every turn, and then being rescued and comforted, calmed, and protected.

We see this type of safety in the psalmist's words above: *shelter, surround, shield.* Hidden in Christ, we have retreated from the imminent danger of sin and grave into the eternal loving care of God.

Often, we think of danger in the physical sense: traversing a dark alley at night, alone. But perhaps we more often experience emotional, relational, or spiritual danger, leading us to distrust others and even ourselves.

When I became aware of just how unseen I was by those closest to me, I began to develop a sense of emotional and relational danger everywhere I turned. My "people-picker" had failed me so miserably that I began questioning what was true and whom I could trust in almost every scenario I encountered. My body would literally seize up, tense, at the least reminder of previous hurt or at the hint of potential hurt—of being misunderstood, ignored, or used. In response, I'd immediately close a protective shell around myself, but every time it was obvious by my racing heart and jumbled mind that I couldn't safeguard anything, much less myself.

Once you've known shocking hurt, you become hypervigilant. You vow you'll never play the fool again, so the hypervigilance masquerades as a helpful friend. But a friend doesn't scream, "Unsafe!" at every turn. A friend doesn't promise you'll be secure as long as you keep playing God—this is Hagar's path of self-dependence.

A friend is a safe place to simply be, hurt and fear and all.

So when the psalmist says that God is our refuge, he's saying there is only one perfect place of emotional, relational, and spiritual safety—it's in the person of Christ himself. He has "refuged" us from the fiery, accusing darts of Satan. He is our ever-present help during suffering.[6] He has "refuged" us from our own sin and its painful condemnation—he is the covering we need in place of our impotent and destructive fig-leaf strategies.

What the psalmist is trying to tell us is that God is safe and we should run to him! It's not a marathon to get to him; he is as close as a breathed prayer or the heart beating in our chest. He waits for our cry, ready to act. To "run to him" is simply to consider him, look to him, call upon him. We can be our full and unvarnished self with him. We can disclose everything to him, and he receives us, bending to listen, prompting us to drain, even to the last drop, our fears and hurts to him.

---

6. Psalm 46:1.

He is a refuge not only because he receives and listens but also because of how he responds. Remember, true seenness involves receiving *and* giving. As he receives our need, look at what he gives: "Grace to you and peace from God our Father and the Lord Jesus Christ. Blessed be the God and Father of our Lord Jesus Christ, the Father of mercies and the God of *all comfort*. He comforts us in all our affliction" (2 Cor. 1:2–4, emphasis added).

God, we're told, is the source of grace, peace, mercy, and comfort. If we're looking for these things—and we are—we will find them as we seek refuge in God. The God of all comfort and mercy acts like an umbrella that protects us from the elements of anxiety, fear, despair, anger, bitterness, and numbness that those who don't seek refuge in God must contend with in the midst of their suffering. As those hidden in Christ, we're not exempted from pain and suffering, but we have God and are protected from these impotent responses.

In other words, we don't have to receive wounds and suffering and then give to ourselves whatever ineffective comfort we can muster. Instead of being left to our own devices, because we're "refuged" in God, we're given comfort.

Comfort, or "consolation" in some Bible translations, means to alleviate or lessen grief, sorrow, or disappointment in our afflictions—the inward pressure we feel that results from difficult circumstances. It also means to strengthen or to come alongside, a word most closely associated in the New Testament with the Holy Spirit: *Paraclete*.

My sons have occasionally been invited to a birthday party in which each guest gets inside their own giant inflatable ball and, alongside their team, attempts to move their ball across the opposing team's goal line. The boys push into one another from inside their inflatable ball, turning every which way as they do, but the blows inflicted against them are softened by the bubble around them. In other words, they have a blast.

When I think of being "refuged" in God, I think of those inflatable balls. Look again at 2 Corinthians 1:2–4 and notice the "surrounding" language and who is involved in the surrounding of the Christian: God the Father, who is sovereign and omniscient, and therefore knows what we need, offers himself as the source of comfort; Christ, who experienced humanity and understands our greatest griefs, opened to us the path of freedom; and the Holy Spirit, who indwells us with strength and upholds us through affliction.

Because we are hidden in Christ, we are figuratively in an inflatable ball. When we experience inner despair from outward circumstances, God lessens our grief, sorrow, and disappointment through his indwelling presence. But we can also think of his strength within us pushing from the inside out, enabling us to endure what we're facing, empowering us to do what in our own human strength we can't do.

This is what it means to be hidden in him.

Secured

In the days I felt most unseen, disregarded by those I trusted most to see and love me, the most comforting place to be was with God, pouring out my heart to him, asking him to vindicate me and show me what was true.

I felt like a wounded animal, wild with emotion and jumpy at anyone's nearness. Over and over I would repeat to myself, "God is safe," which helped calm me and remind me to turn to him, even if I couldn't find the words to fit my wounds or the words I found were the same ones I'd already said countless times.

He didn't leave me when I kept saying the same things over and over or when I said hard things that didn't sound very Christian or when I screamed at the top of my lungs. He didn't tell me to dry my tears or hush my sobbing. He didn't shush or shame or give up on me, even when I went off swirling in my anger and disappointment at what he'd allowed, when I couldn't do anything resembling any sort of faith except for letting him hold onto me.

I had so much to sort through and process, but I can tell you now as I reflect on that time, I was "refuged" as I muddled my way through. I was safe to ask the hard questions of God, like, "Where were you, God?" And, "Can I trust you will protect me in the future, God?" I was comforted by his character, presence, promises, and his Word. Though I longed to be through the process from the first day I encountered suffering, he was a Good Shepherd in walking me slowly through the shadow of the valley of death. When I wanted to lash out or vent my self-righteous anger, I found correction and solace in knowing my Refuge is also my just Judge.[7]

I was inside the inflatable ball: the blows were softened by his indwelling presence, and I was strengthened from the inside out, compelled to act contrary to my flesh and in tandem with his ways.

I couldn't have gotten through that time without knowing God is a God Who Sees and who has "seen to it." He was so

---

7. 2 Peter 2:23.

deeply personal, so deeply patient, and so deeply proactive that I could do nothing else but entrust myself to him.

How insightful for us that it wasn't Hagar's obedience to return that changed the course of this family's story. It wasn't Abraham's faith or Sarah's faithlessness in giving Hagar to Abram. What changed the course of this family's story was God's faithfulness, demonstrated in the birth of Isaac—the firstborn son of promise.

God is faithful and keeps all his promises. He holds on, and he does it with a firm and gentle hand. How does he do it just right, never harming us while also applying pressure, doing things that are confusing to us at the time but later turn out to be for our good? Like requiring Abraham to take Isaac to the top of the mountain. Like requiring his Son to do the same. I don't know.

But we don't have to know.

We're not meant to be security guards over our own life.

We're the ones being secured.

We're refuged in Christ.

For Further Reflection

1. Why is it such a good thing to be "hidden" in Christ? As you consider this for yourself—that you are hidden in Christ—does that speak to any of the hurts you've experienced in your unseenness?

2. For those who have put on fig leaves and sought visibility through idolatrous means, he has "seen to it" that our sins are forgiven when we come to him by faith, seeking restoration. What

flimsy fig leaves are you prone to still cover yourself with? What does Christ's sacrifice say about you and about those fig leaves?

3. How would you define what it means to be seen by God?

Part Four

HE SEES AND ACTS
ON YOUR BEHALF

Chapter 7

HE SEES SO HE INTERCEDES

I n the pain of my unseenness, knowing I was safe with God, I began to ask him many pointed questions: *Where were you, God? How could you have let me be so painfully disregarded? Did you see what was happening and attempt to intervene on my behalf? Does my pain matter to you?*

After sitting for so long in Hagar's story and letting her take me back to Sarah and her child of promise, I not only began to ask pointed questions, but I also began to zoom out to look at all of Scripture and explore how God acts when he sees his children. Surprisingly, I found some of my own questions voiced by people in the Bible.

That spring, on Easter Sunday, Kyle preached about Lazarus being raised from the dead, concluding his sermon with Jesus's ultimate triumph over sin and death. I struggled to attend to the sermon because as soon as Kyle started reading the text, I became fixated on Mary and Martha instead of on Lazarus or, for the moment, Jesus:

> Now a man was sick—Lazarus from Bethany, the village of Mary and her sister Martha. Mary was the one who anointed the Lord with perfume and wiped his feet with her hair, and it was her brother Lazarus who was sick. So the sisters sent a message to him: "Lord, the one you love is sick."
>
> When Jesus heard it, he said, "This sickness will not end in death but is for the glory of God, so that the Son of God may be glorified through it." Now Jesus loved Martha, her sister, and Lazarus. So when he heard that he was sick, he stayed two more days in the place where he was. (John 11:1–6)

Through messengers, Mary and Martha told Jesus Lazarus was sick, and Jesus didn't respond. Instead, he stayed where he was.

They didn't make a specific request of Jesus, but we can read between the lines of their message: *Will you come for us?* They were surely frightened that their beloved brother was near death. But Jesus didn't go to them, explaining to his listeners that he was *intentionally* delaying. His delay, he said, would ultimately bring glory to God.

I'd heard this story a thousand times before that Easter Sunday and, each time, had focused on the end—the glory of God shown in the resurrection of Lazarus. But this time I thought about Mary and Martha and the pain they endured. I wondered how Jesus's delay glorified God, not merely through the life of Lazarus but also in the lives of Mary and Martha? How could one verse proclaim Jesus loved Martha and Mary and the next say, "So . . . he stayed . . . where he was" instead of "He rushed to their sides and healed Lazarus"?

Because while Jesus stayed where he was, Lazarus died.

Days passed, and as their friends gathered to grieve Lazarus and comfort Mary and Martha, someone mentioned that Jesus was headed their way. At this news, Mary didn't move, but Martha got up and ran to meet him on the road, likely with tears streaming down her face.

When she found him on the road, the first thing she said was, "Lord, if you had been here, my brother wouldn't have died" (John 11:21). What sort of inflection or emotion could have been in her voice as she spoke? Was it a confession of belief or a hard question disguised as a statement?

Later Mary also went to find Jesus and, when she did, she repeated her sister's phrase: "Lord, if you had been here, my brother wouldn't have died!" (v. 32). Whatever her exact tone was, it apparently called for an exclamation point.

Finally, the gathering crowd joined in Mary and Martha's refrain: "Couldn't he who opened the blind man's eyes also have kept this man from dying?" (v. 37).

In previous readings of the story, my eyes so focused on the glorious ending, I hadn't ever imagined the confusion Mary and Martha must have felt as this story unfolded or the emotional roller coaster they were taken on. This time, however, I saw it: they were women who had experienced a sense of disregard and had asked Jesus the same kinds of questions I was asking! *Where were you, God? You could have prevented this pain I'm feeling, God! If only you'd come . . .*

Kyle continued preaching about Lazarus, but my mind remained on Mary and Martha. I felt their anguish as if I were walking with them to find Jesus on the road. They seemed to then beckon me from inside their story to turn toward Jesus and observe his responses to their questions.

With Martha he didn't explain his delay. He simply asked for her trust, and she gave it. She believed, she said, he would cause her brother to rise in the final resurrection. Jesus took her hope and fulfilled it in a way Martha couldn't have imagined.

In response to Mary, Jesus saw her tears and immediately became emotional himself or, as Scripture says, "deeply moved in his spirit and troubled" (v. 33). He was angry and upset at the effects of sin, at the reality that those he loved should feel such grief and pain, and at the far-reaching work of death.

Notice there is a second delay in the story. Jesus delayed resolving the pain and discomfort of those he loved to enter into Mary's grief and weep with her.

He saw tears in the eyes of someone he loved, so he himself cried.

After viewing Lazarus's body, again, he wept.

And then he interceded.

> Then Jesus, deeply moved again, came to the tomb. It was a cave, and a stone was lying against it. "Remove the stone," Jesus said.
>
> Martha, the dead man's sister, told him, "Lord, there is already a stench because he has been dead four days."
>
> Jesus said to her, "Didn't I tell you that if you believed you would see the glory of God?"

So they removed the stone. Then Jesus raised
his eyes and said, "Father, I thank you that you
heard me. I know that you always hear me, but
because of the crowd standing here I said this,
so that they may believe you sent me." After he
said this, he shouted with a loud voice, "Lazarus,
come out!" The dead man came out bound
hand and foot with linen strips and with his face
wrapped in a cloth. Jesus said to them, "Unwrap
him and let him go." (vv. 38–44)

Notice the "seeing" language throughout this encounter.
When Jesus saw their grief, he also knew with his heart their pain
and anguish. He registered the effects of sin and death. And when
he saw, he acted—by bringing to life what was dead.

What struck me that Easter Sunday is that in the space
between death and resurrection, Jesus purposefully let Mary and
Martha (and the crowd) hear him talking to God the Father,
essentially giving them a behind-the-scenes look at the relationship between God the Father and God the Son.

Then the unexpected happened. Martha believed Jesus would
raise Lazarus from the dead in the final resurrection, but until the
moment Lazarus walked out of the grave in his graveclothes, she
shooed Jesus away from the tomb, trying to protect him from the
stench of death.

But he had to show who he was! He was giving her what she
needed most—not protection from pain, but rather he was giving her himself. And although he took Mary and Martha on a
wild ride, in the end, it was a wild ride toward glory. He received
glory specifically in Martha's life through her belief. What she'd

expressed before Lazarus's resurrection—belief in Jesus as the resurrection and the life and hope for life after death—was confirmed for her right before her eyes. Think about what that does for a heart!

God Isn't a Snowplow Parent

Within the week, Jesus would enter Jerusalem on a donkey. Days after that, he would be crucified—the Resurrection and the Life put to death. Days after that, he would be in a tomb, wrapped in graveclothes like Lazarus had been. Don't you know that Mary and Martha revisited their question: *Where were you, God? If you had been here, Jesus wouldn't have died.*

Though we don't have record of their responses or actions following the crucifixion, we can imagine they called upon the belief that had been confirmed by Christ at Lazarus's resurrection—*God would bring to life what was dead.*

God is *always* bringing to life what is dead. When we are wondering, *Where were you, God?*, he doesn't always give us answers or explanations, but as Jesus did with Mary and Martha, he gives us more of himself.

If Jesus had come right away, would Martha's faith have been strengthened in just the right way that she could withstand what would come later? Would she have known with such certainty that Jesus was the Son of God, the Resurrection and the Life, and be able to boldly proclaim him after his own resurrection and ascension?

When I read one verse proclaiming Jesus loved Martha and Mary and the next telling me, "So . . . he stayed . . . where he was," I think of parenting and how badly I want to protect my boys from all difficulty and suffering. A term has developed around this modern idea of parenting taken to extremes: *snowplow parenting.* A snowplow parent is one who seeks to remove all obstacles from a child's path so they don't experience pain, failure, or discomfort.[1] But the best advice I ever received from an older mom was never to rescue my children from a challenge or obstacle that could, if they navigate it on their own with my presence and support, cultivate their confidence in what they're able to face, grow their conflict skills, and deepen their trust in God. This mentor mom asked me to consider how I had grown in faith and wisdom. It was, of course, through challenges and difficulty, just as Scripture speaks of what is a possible outcome of our suffering: "We know that affliction produces endurance, endurance produces proven character, and proven character produces hope" (Rom. 5:3–4).

God is not a snowplow parent, and we see this clearly in how Jesus responded to Mary and Martha. He doesn't always protect us from difficult circumstances, but he always uses those difficult circumstances to build our faith muscles and to grow in us a deeper experiential knowledge of who he is. He doesn't leave us to navigate our difficult circumstances on our own, but as a good Father, he patiently walks alongside us and helps us as we go.

No good parent takes pleasure in their child's pain; similarly, God is not unaffected emotionally by our suffering. We need only to observe how Jesus entered into the experience with Mary and Martha to know that when we grieve, he grieves. When we suffer,

---

1. Dan Brennan, "What Is Snowplow Parenting?" WebMD, April 23, 2023, https://www.webmd.com/parenting/what-is-snowplow-parenting#:~:text=Snowplow%20parenting%2C%20also%20called%20lawnmower,pain%2C%20failure%2C%20or%20discomfort.

he feels it with us. He willingly endures pain with us because, in the end, he knows the difficult circumstance will become a milestone of his faithfulness we can recall when we come upon additional difficult circumstances in our journey called life.

In other words, he is giving us a gift that will last a lifetime.

Someone Is Talking about You

I needed the Lazarus story on that particular Easter Sunday, and I need it still. I needed to see Jesus and to observe what his eyes observed—where he looked, how he responded to what he saw, and how he acted on behalf of those in his sight.

In John 11, it was as if I saw him seeing me and seeing the circumstances of my own life. I, too, felt desperate in a situation I believed God could have prevented. I, too, wondered why he hadn't come for me. However, as Jesus cried for and with Mary and Martha, I knew he felt my sadness and entered into my particular grief. As he strengthened Martha's resolve and trust in him, I sensed he would do the same for me if I would only persist in faith. And as he vocally interceded for Lazarus and for Mary and Martha, I considered how Scripture says he intercedes for me: "Christ Jesus is the one who died, but even more, has been raised; he also is at the right hand of God and intercedes for us" (Rom. 8:34).

I'd spent a lifetime considering Jesus's past work on the cross and through his resurrection and all its thousands of implications, but I'd never considered Jesus's *present* work and its implications: he is right now, at this moment, sitting beside God the Father and interceding for you and for me. He is speaking to God the Father about us, petitioning for us. Hebrews 7:25 repeats Jesus's current job description but adds the word *always*: "He *always* lives to intercede for [those who come to God through him]" (emphasis added).

Friend, he is always praying for you! He is praying for you right now!

What do you think he is talking to God about regarding you?

The language for intercession in Hebrews 7:25 mirrors the language used in the Old Testament to describe what the high priest did for his people. Just as the high priest was the human representative who entered the presence of God and made atonement for himself and the sins of his people, we're reminded of how Jesus took on flesh (but did not sin) and, therefore, identifies himself with your humanity. He knows what it's like to experience the emotional wear and tear of being human, so as he's interceding for you, he's translating to God the Father what you feel, think, and navigate as a human being.

Rather than merely requesting something, intercession implies intervention, which is fitting, because instead of an Old Testament high priest who had to continually make offerings to cover sin, Jesus made the once-for-all offering of himself as the sacrifice for sin.[2] He's gone to the furthest extent he can for you, so of course he wants his work to benefit you! Thus, he intervenes, calling on his boundless capital with God the Father to ensure the full benefit of his work on the cross and over the grave is applied to your heart, mind, and circumstances. He knows the extent of his saving power, so as he's interceding for you, he's calling on

---

2. Kenneth S. Wuest, *Wuest's Word Studies from the Greek New Testament: For the English Reader*, vol. 10 (Grand Rapids, MI: Eerdmans, 1997), 138.

God to cause his grace and mercy to permeate every part of your life.

Jesus acts as your intermediary, pushing your prayers up toward God and communicating God's will and character down toward you.

When we feel forgotten and unsure, we don't always know how to pray, but this inability to come up with words and requests doesn't hinder Christ's work at all. Instead, our inability to form words around our need only invites the Holy Spirit to join in all the intercession: "In the same way the Spirit also helps us in our weakness, because we do not know what to pray for as we should, but the Spirit himself intercedes for us with inexpressible groanings" (Rom. 8:26).

In this iteration of the word *intercedes*, the Spirit is said to go to meet God the Father for consultation, conversation, or supplication.[3] The language the Spirit uses is unknown to us—described here as inexpressible groanings—but it is a language God hears and understands, and they are prayers that always align with God's will for us.

You, my friend, have the entire Godhead talking together about how much good they want for you and how they're going to act to bring that good about. Even better, your intercessors know exactly what you need, so they know exactly what to request of God the Father.

3. Marvin R. Vincent, *Word Studies in the New Testament*, vol. 3 (New York: Charles Scribner's Sons, 1887), 95.

Only One Who Understands

One of the five categories of unseenness we named in part 1 of this book was being or feeling misunderstood by others. We described this type of unseenness as life circumstances that make us feel "other," when few know or understand the nuances and intricacies of your specific life circumstance and what burdens you privately carry as a result.

All of us at some point in life, by nature of being a human in a fallen world, will experience being misunderstood. Perhaps you're navigating something right now that has left you feeling alone and "other."

To know that Jesus and the Holy Spirit intercede and intervene is a deep comfort when you also know that God is a God Who Sees and knows everything about you, including the circumstance no one else seems to understand or is willing to acknowledge. He knows your heart, and "the LORD has heard the sound of [your] weeping" (Ps. 6:8).

When I was a young mom, we received a difficult diagnosis for one of our sons that sent me into a downward spiral of grief.

One of the most difficult aspects of navigating and processing my son's diagnosis was being around other kids who did not share that diagnosis. I noticed everything about those kids that was different from my child, and while I didn't wish away my son, I wished away the reality of my circumstances.

Eventually, the sadness and grief developed into bitterness. Sitting at the playground, watching moms I didn't know push their kids on the swings, I internally shot my bitter arrows directly into their hearts. Why did they have it easy? Why did my child have such a hard road ahead but theirs didn't? I envied them and refused to believe that, in fact, no one has it easy.

Worse, I shot my bitter arrows at friends and family, who showed me so much love and support. It didn't matter what they said or did to encourage or help me. It was never right or enough because nothing they said or did could erase my pain or alter my circumstances. I felt utterly and completely alone, like I was the only person on the planet who was going through these specific circumstances.

And so the bitter root grew wildly out of control, resulting in my own isolation and compounded grief.

The truth is, I *was* the only person going through these specific circumstances. No one else could be me, and no one else could know the inner workings of my heart. No one else could be my son, with his unique personality, gifts, and needs. No one else lived in the unique intersection of my individual and family context.

I was beyond bothered that no one could fully enter my grief because I felt sure my pain would be validated or would ease if someone just understood me. So I shot my bitter arrows while fruitlessly waiting for someone to come along who saw what I was going through and say, "I understand completely."

During that year, I providentially read Proverbs 14:10: "The heart knows its own bitterness, and no outsider shares in its joy."

The truth of this verse jumped out at me as both deeply convicting and as a beacon of hope. The wording is a bit difficult to understand, but it tells us that we have feelings, both joyful and sorrowful, that ultimately cannot be understood by another person. Sometimes we don't even understand those feelings ourselves, and, therefore, we can't fully express how we feel. When we try, when we lay it all out before another person, we still aren't fully understood. There are limits to human understanding, and if we rely solely on human love and understanding for our comfort, we will quickly grow bitter and hard and will distance ourselves from others in our disappointment.

Like I did.

But "there is one who sticks closer than a brother" (Prov. 18:24 ESV). When I realized there was One who understood everything I was going through, One who would never misunderstand me, and One who knew me better than I knew myself, I was finally able to release my family and friends from the pressure of my expectations that they'd carry the full weight of my grief. I was also finally able to rest in the comfort the Lord had been giving me all along.

What is your current difficult circumstance that has left you feeling unseen? Where has frustration at being misunderstood crept in and affected your relationships? Are you looking to others to respond in a way that only God can?

Now is the time to turn to the One who sticks closer than any friend, sister, parent, or pastor. God sees you. He understands. And he looks after you in a way no one else can.

An Advance Worker

That Easter Sunday was a turning point for me as I processed the pain of being unseen. I found an answer to the question I'd been asking over and over and that God had so patiently received each time. *God, where were you? If only you'd come.*

He was there all along. He hadn't taken a coffee break or checked out but rather had taken it all in—not one detail escaped his sight. At the same time, he'd allowed me to experience the pain of it because he had a plan for the pain. Like an exacting surgeon, he'd made a cut—not so deep as to kill but deep enough to do a work of healing in an area of my heart I didn't know needed healing. All along, when things were happening I couldn't see, he'd interceded for me in advance, working to turn dead things into alive things—things inside of me and in my marriage, things that I didn't know were dead or dying.

God is an advance worker, going before us to prepare good from the hard. I know this because in the story of Mary, Martha, and Lazarus, when Jesus prayed, he said something peculiar to God the Father: "Father, I thank you that you heard me."

Not, "Father, please hear me," as if the miraculous work of resurrection could then commence, but rather, "You heard me." Past tense.

When did Jesus first intercede for Lazarus and, therefore, Mary and Martha? He must have prayed an unrecorded prayer in advance of that moment, perhaps when he first received the message about Lazarus's sickness, or perhaps even upon his first encounters with the siblings. This advanced petition was a prayer Mary and Martha knew nothing about, but he was interceding in advance of their need.

This is your God, the God Who Sees. He sees in advance. He's aware in advance. And he's interceded for you in advance, all the way back to the resurrection, even further back to the cross, and even further back to his recorded prayers before Jesus went to the cross.[4]

Just think of the countless words the Godhead has exchanged about you in the millennia between then and now.

As I asked God, "Where were you?," I took great comfort in discovering how Jesus is my Intercessor, my Intervener. I realized, too, that he'd not only spoken to God about me, but he'd also spoken to people about me. He'd convicted others on my behalf. He'd nudged others to come alongside and encourage me, even when they didn't know the details of my pain. He'd empowered his Body, the church, to edify me in ways they will never know were significant to me.

In addition, knowing Jesus and the Holy Spirit intercede for me emboldened my own prayers. I could join in the chorus of prayer, making my requests known to God.[5]

You, too, can join in the chorus. But first, slow down and know the gaze of God. Follow his eyes as we've followed Jesus's eyes toward Mary and Martha and notice that he sees you. If you're weeping, he weeps with you. If you're looking for resurrection, he's the Resurrection and the Life. As he sees you, he intercedes for you, just as he has before you knew you needed his prayers.

For Further Reflection

1. Have you experienced something that led you to ask, "Where were you, God?" As you've read this chapter and have observed Jesus with Mary and Martha, take a moment to consider Jesus

4. John 17:20–26.
5. Philippians 4:6–7.

being with you in your difficult experience (because he was there). How do you think he experienced that with you? What might he have felt for you or with you? How might he have experienced the situation or person who hurt you?

2. In the chapter, you read, "[God] doesn't always protect us from difficult circumstances, but he always uses those difficult circumstances to build our faith muscles and to grow in us a deeper experiential knowledge of who he is." Have you found this to be true? If so, how?

3. In your unseenness, where has frustration at being misunderstood crept in and affected your relationships? Are you looking to others to respond in a way that only God can?

4. How does Jesus's present work of being an intercessor for you speak to you or provide you comfort and strength?

Chapter 8

HE SEES SO HE DELIVERS

O ne of the requests I continually made to God during the years I felt invisible was that he would allow me to use the gifts he'd given me within our local church. Through writing, podcasting, and speaking, my work often allowed me the privilege of encouraging the global church, but inside my own church, I often felt overlooked for who I was and how I wanted to serve, while at the same time laden with expectation to be what I wasn't and to serve in ways I didn't want to serve.

As I described in a previous chapter, in helping my husband plant the church, I'd given everything I could give to ensure the church was established and healthy, and while my heart stayed completely invested throughout the fourteen years we were there, I struggled to find significant ways to be involved without over-stepping or stepping on toes. My heart ached with good desires, but my ideas and offers mostly went unheard. Instead, I was told I made leaders feel threatened, and my pleas to my husband, who had authority and opportunity to help, fell on deaf ears—or, at least, ears that heard countless ideas every day and struggled to wade through them.

I was on an island, and I knew it. Attending church and engaging people became an act of obedience rather than a joy. I will say, the Lord sustained me and gave me what I needed not just to endure but to love and engage people. But life started to feel like I was slogging through mud. Or, as I'd later describe that season, as if my clothes no longer fit comfortably.

I tried to be patient, as people told me to be. I tried to believe the best of others and support them, even when I didn't feel supported myself. I examined my motives for wanting to serve, and the Lord showed me at times that I needed this unending season of humbling. I'm thankful for his refining, but when I look back at that time now, I see that I generally had good desires, as well as a Holy Spirit-backed compulsion to do what God had made me to do. The desires simply had no outlet.

Perhaps you've been there or are there currently. You have a desire to be married, or a desire for a friend, or a desire for relief, or a desire to do with your life what feels like worship when you do it. None of these are bad desires, but when these desires have no forthcoming outlet, it can be extremely challenging and can even begin to elicit shame—we feel bad for having good desires.

That's what happened to me. I began to question myself, figuring the blame for the desire not coming to fruition was somehow mine. *Perhaps I don't see myself correctly,* I thought. *Perhaps I do not actually have those gifts and I'm prideful to think I do,* I thought. *Perhaps I think I'm something I'm not and the other person's perspective on me* (that I'm threatening, for example) *is the more accurate one*, I thought. *Perhaps I am misunderstanding the situation and God himself,* I thought. *Perhaps I'm simply too much.*

And yet the Holy Spirit would not relent. God seemed to be pushing me forward into a human brick wall, which was extremely confusing.

I lived with this confusion for years, serving him as best I could in the margins.

Self-Disregard

In the last chapter, we explored the category of unseenness I've labeled "being misunderstood." In this chapter, we'll explore two more: disregard and unfulfilled desires. Disregard, we've said, is a lack of attention, consideration, or respect. To be disregarded is essentially to be ignored. I know a thing or two about that.

But there is one additional category of unseenness we must address, and that is *self-disregard*. Self-disregard is a learned behavior that develops out of disregard. If others think we're unworthy of respect or regard, we begin to think and act like they're right. We come to believe we're unworthy, that something must be wrong on our end.

Self-disregard comes in various forms. It can be a chosen invisibility; perhaps parts of our history have resulted in shame, guilt, or confusion that we don't want people to know about, so we hide those parts in the shadows.

Self-disregard can also involve an unhealthy diminishing in the name of godliness. As I look back at my own life, I notice this type of unhealthy diminishing, where to be legitimized and valuable was to conform to and ensure the needs, desires, and successes of those around me. I'd chosen this because I'd believed this was what was expected of me as a wife, mom, pastor's wife, and Christian woman. To act on a God-given compulsion to do anything outside of certain parameters became a scary and even a questionable thing. Remaining diminished is far easier than wrestling with the notion of stepping out into the unknown and potentially receiving negative feedback.

A person living in their own chosen unseenness may even wonder, *Is it right to want to be seen?*

We must not confuse self-disregard and self-denial. Jesus taught us to deny ourselves to follow him, but he didn't teach self-disregard. Self-denial is active obedience to Christ that also requires a deep knowledge and assurance of who we are in Christ and the gifts he's given us by the Holy Spirit. We offer all of who we are and the gifts he's given us to his service, and we are willing to use everything we have for his sake rather than our own. At the heart of self-denial is a deep confidence in God because the engine and goal is God's glory rather than self-glory. In other words, it's not just visibility for visibility's sake. We experience joy and satisfaction in God, whether he has us serving visibly or not.

Self-disregard, ironically, worries incessantly about visibility. *Will I be seen as pushy? Am I too much? Am I not enough? What will people think?* Somehow visibility is seen as wrong and ungodly when it is, in fact, a type of false humility. We don't respect ourselves as image bearers or trust that God may be leading or prompting us to step out in faith and are instead driven by fear, timidity, and a need for approval. We can only trust what others say about who we are and what we're to do, not what God says.

Self-disregard, in other words, makes us believe we aren't worthy of being seen or heard. It is inordinately consumed with visibility, dismissing the idea that any private obedience or unseen service is of value.

We are often dissatisfied while trying to convince ourselves to be satisfied.

That is exactly the spot I found myself in. I felt unworthy to be heard, and I did not trust the Spirit in me that perhaps my desires were directly in step with his will. Never in a million years would I have believed that anyone around me may not have been reflecting back to me what was true and right and good.

I was disregarding my own self. I needed deliverance out of the craziness, but I remember thinking that if I just found and confessed my own sin, I could remove what was hindering me, or if I just denied myself more and highlighted others, or if I just kept persevering in the dynamic I existed in, it would somehow get better.

I tried repeatedly to create my own deliverance through these efforts. In fact, almost acting as a flailing response, I pushed my performance button more and more, becoming a compulsive doer, an overfunctioner, and an always-on-the-move person. If I'd been asked to tell who I was at that point in my life, all my responses would have had some sort of production attached to them. The strategy of overfunctioning served me well for so long, but I found myself inordinately weary and lacking connection with myself and others.

There is a stark contrast between self-deliverance and God's deliverance. Self-deliverance is impotent and dissatisfactory, often temporary and filled with land mines. God's deliverance is powerful and lasting, a type of work on our behalf that leaves us slack-jawed.

For me, God's deliverance out of those years began with an unexpected word.

Wait.

That was not the word I wanted to hear.

Fearing the Future When the Present Is Hard

Another question I found myself repeatedly asking during my season of being unseen, especially related to my unfulfilled desires was, "God, can I actually trust you?"

When God has acted in ways that are confusing, such as allowing prolonged difficult circumstances or relationships, we're tempted to develop a dread of the future. What if he allows difficult things for us in the future? What if our circumstances never get better?

We all face doubts. Sometimes I doubt if God is there at all, but most of the time my doubt is more like wariness. I wonder if God can truly be trusted, especially regarding my future, so I sort of hedge my bets. *I'll trust you somewhat, Lord and, also, I'll worry.* My bet-hedging of choice was, as I mentioned previously, compulsive doing—believing somehow I could work my way out of my difficult circumstances.

We all struggle at some level with worry over the future. And when we worry, we tend to try to control and plan so that we can avert danger or negative results.

Think for a moment about your deepest concern or unfulfilled desires in your unseenness. What is keeping you up at night? What are you worried about? What are you attempting to control? What do you fear about your circumstances or the future? Keep your concerns in mind as we turn toward a specific people in a specific time who were slogging through the mud, so to speak, and desperately desired deliverance out of their circumstances. We have much we can learn and apply based on what God says to them.

The specific people in a specific time were the people of God in exile. God allowed and authored the discipline of exile for his people because they had rejected him and instead sought their peace and protection in military power and self-sufficiency. They'd been exiled to Babylon, a pagan nation bent on destroying God's people.

Prior to where we'll pick up in their story, God had promised he would make a way for them to return to their homeland and that this would foreshadow a greater hope: that God himself would come to walk among them and shepherd them. Notably, God made this promise through his prophet Isaiah *before God's people even went into exile*. (Another example of God being an advance worker!)

As exiles in a foreign land, they'd lost everything that was significant to them. Their nation and temple had been destroyed. They'd lost their sense of cultural identity. Their children were being raised under widespread pagan influence.

They were a people in need of deliverance, but they lived in a time of yet-to-be-fulfilled promises and unfulfilled desires.

What would you think and feel if you were in this situation? I would feel abandoned by God, wondering if his promises were empty. Even if I did hold out hope for deliverance, I imagine it would be difficult to foresee a scenario of how it could even happen. Deliverance so often seems impossible when we most need it.

Being a God Who Sees and a God who knows, God spoke to his people through Isaiah, and he emphasized that Isaiah was to herald his message far and wide. God wanted everyone stuck in exile to hear—the destitute, the parents worried for the future of their children, the homesick, the lonely, the oppressed, those unjustly treated, those who had lost their professional identities, those who had far more questions than answers, and those who held a laundry list of hurts and regrets. His words are recorded in Scripture, so he also wants *us* to hear. These words are for everyone, which is significant because everyone is going to be tempted to think their situation or circumstance lies outside the truth of these words.

God wants everyone to know who he is because his character is the answer to the primary doubts that filled the exile's fears and that also fill our worries about the future.

His Words to the Worriers and Doubters

We find God's words to the exiles in Isaiah 40:12–31. He speaks first to the worriers and doubters, who were perhaps thinking, *This situation we're in is bigger than God. Our circumstances are out of his reach, and, therefore, we're on our own.* Perhaps you can relate?

To them, God said: "Who has measured the waters in the hollow of his hand or marked off the heavens with the span of his hand? Who has gathered the dust of the earth in a measure or weighed the mountains on a balance and the hills on the scales?" (Isa. 40:12).

We may be tempted to read God's tone as impatient or even angry, as if he's saying, "Guys, could you just get it together

already?" But God is acting as a Father who first disciplined and
then comforted his children.

If you have a child, consider a time when your child was dis-
traught or worried. You probably pulled him or her onto your lap
and said, "Sweet child, I've got you. You have nothing to worry
about." That is essentially what God did with his people. He
sought to reassure them: *I've got you. You have nothing to worry
about. Do you think this situation is the one situation that is too big
for me to handle?*

The worriers and doubters were thinking in terms of measurements. In their estimation, their situation was too big and
God was too small. So God, using a series of rhetorical questions,
asked them to reconsider their measurements:

> *Who has measured the waters?*
>
> *Who has marked off the heavens with a span?*
> (A span is the distance between the end of the
> thumb and the little finger when the hand is fully
> extended.)
>
> *Who has gathered the dust of the earth?*
>
> *Who has weighed the mountains and hills on the
> scales?*

There is only one answer to each of these rhetorical questions:
God. Not the Babylonian king, the most powerful and authorita-
tive person they could think of. Not the people in exile, questioning where God was and if he was able to do what he'd said he'd
do. Only God is and can ever be the answer to these rhetorical
questions.

And not only is the only answer God, but notice how God measures: with his hands. He holds the oceans and measures the heavens and picks up the mountains and hills to put them on a scale. The children's song is theological truth: he's truly got the whole world in his hands.

The expanses mentioned here are the largest elements of creation we can perceive, but God says they are small in relation to him, and he says there is no place, from ocean to sky, from dust to mountain, where his hands can't reach and affect.

The imagery of hands is something to consider. When I think of hands, I think of tenderness and affection. And I think of work. God conveyed to his people that he is for them and was at work in the circumstances that concerned them.

So for the worriers and doubters who were perhaps thinking, *The situation we're in is bigger than God. Perhaps this is the one situation that is out of his reach, and, therefore, we're on our own,* God essentially said, "I am not just bigger; I'm far bigger than your circumstances. I've got this. You don't have any basis for worry."

God's Words for the Controllers

But the worriers and doubters who were prone to trying to control might have then piped up, because perhaps they were thinking, *That's great that God is bigger than my situation, but it seems as if God doesn't know what he's doing, so I need to help him. He may be working, but he isn't aware of all the details, and he isn't responding the way I wish he would, so I need to tell him how best to handle these circumstances.*

Again, God asks rhetorical questions: "Who has directed the Spirit of the LORD, or who gave him counsel? Who did he consult? Who gave him understanding and taught him the paths of justice? Who taught him knowledge and showed him the way of understanding?" (Isa. 40:13–14).

The answer to each of these rhetorical questions is *no one*. No one has instructed, directed, or counseled God because he is the source of these things. He is perfect counsel. He is perfect understanding. He is perfect justice. He is perfect knowledge. Any understanding and knowledge we have flows down from the source. There is no higher authority or more original source.

God was essentially saying, "Do you think I don't understand what's happening? Do you think I don't know how to fix it? Do you think I don't understand what justice is for you in this situation?"

We think God doesn't see, or perhaps he's not engaged enough to see it all. We think he couldn't possibly figure out how to get us to where he wants us or where he wants those we love, so it's up to us to figure it out and to make it happen. We think he doesn't understand justice, so we're entitled to hold grudges and make people pay for what they've done to us. We want to tell God what to do and how to do it.

In thinking again about size and measurements, we attempt to place ourselves in the highest place of authority. No wonder anxiety so often accompanies our attempt to control—it feels as if the whole world is in our hands and that our God is small and incompetent.

So to the worriers and doubters who were prone to control, those who thought, *God doesn't know what he's doing, so I need to tell him how best to handle these circumstances,* God essentially said, "I am far bigger and far wiser. I've got this. You have no basis for your worry."

God's Words to the Despairing

But then the worriers and doubters who were prone to despair spoke up because they were perhaps thinking, *He is not in authority over all things, especially over those who don't submit to him and whose actions have affected me or continue to affect me. Therefore, I'm helpless and hopeless.*

Whose actions were affecting the exiles? The Babylonians, a pagan nation ruled by a pagan king. And they were powerhouses in that moment of history. The exiles were under the authority of those who didn't care about them, didn't bow their knee to God, and who had taken everything from them.

God has something to say about those who oppressed his people: "Look, the nations are like a drop in a bucket; they are considered as a speck of dust on the scales; he lifts up the islands like fine dust. Lebanon's cedars are not enough for fuel, or its animals enough for a burnt offering. All the nations are as nothing before him; they are considered by him as empty nothingness" (Isa. 40:15–17).

Again, God told the exiles to think in terms of correct size and measurements. "The nations seem big to you," God said, "but even when they're put all together, with all their power and might and wealth, I am in fact still bigger. And not just a little bigger. I am so much bigger and more powerful that they appear like a piece of dust or a drop of water."

Those who cowered at the might and authority of pagan kings and nations were forced to reconsider their doubt that God didn't have authority over those who oppressed them. In fact, God essentially said, "I am in authority over everything. You are not without hope. There is no basis for worry about those in human authority over you."

Notice that so far Isaiah has first described a God who holds the world in his hands—he is under all of creation, holding it up. Then he described a God who is the source of all things, so he is above all of creation, and any good we experience flows down from him. Finally, he described God as above those who are around and above us.

Under. Above. Around. Is there any direction we can go or any situation we find ourselves in where God is not there and where God is not able?

What Option Do We Have If We Don't Trust God?

Through rhetorical questions and vivid word images, Isaiah spoke God's words clearly to the exiles, asking them three primary questions:

> *Do you think your circumstances are too big or too complex for God?*

> *Do you think God doesn't have wisdom and knowledge enough to know exactly what you need?*

> *Do you think God doesn't have authority over everything and everyone affecting you?*

As we navigate unseenness, these are good questions for us to consider as well. Because if we don't believe God can take care of us, then we must do it. If God can't do it, we should be worried and fearful. If God can't do it, we're left attributing power and authority and wisdom to lesser things, and those things become our gods.

We become our own god.

Other people become our god, and we demand they respond the way we want them to: see us and validate us.

Perfect circumstances become our god.

Others, self, and circumstances loom larger in our measurements, and our eyes are shifted off the one, true God.

Isaiah had some choice words about where this leads: "With whom will you compare God? What likeness will you set up for comparison with him? An idol?—something that a smelter casts and a metalworker plates with gold and makes silver chains for? A poor person contributes wood for a pedestal that will not rot. He looks for a skilled craftsman to set up an idol that will not fall over" (Isa. 40:18–20).

Isaiah mocked the manufacturing of idols, which the people of Judah participated in. He described how the wealthy had their idols overlaid with gold. The poor couldn't afford gold, but that didn't stop them: they chose to make theirs out of wood rather than go without.

The idol described in these verses merely sat—impotent, unmoving, and uncaring—while God is described as tender, engaged, compassionate, powerful, thinking, creating, and using his authority wisely.

Most people don't make statues that they bow down to in worship, although that is certainly happening in parts of the world. So, what are our idols? Anything other than God that we measure as more worthy of our affections and to which we look for peace, comfort, help, hope, or salvation.

How do we know we've replaced God? Idolatry leads to fear, and fear leads to defensiveness, anxiety, control, anger, and despair. For example, if a person is my idol and they disappoint me or I feel insecure in our relationship, I'm going to fear losing them, get angry at the slights I feel, and do things to try to control their behavior.

But there isn't anyone or anything that we can put the full weight of our life upon aside from God. There isn't anyone or anything like him, who is bigger than our circumstances, who holds authority over the world, and who meets our needs at the deepest soul level.

That's where Isaiah goes next:

> Do you not know? Have you not heard? Has it not been declared to you from the beginning? Have you not considered the foundations of the earth? God is enthroned above the circle of the earth; its inhabitants are like grasshoppers. He stretches out the heavens like thin cloth and spreads them out like a tent to live in. He reduces princes to nothing and makes judges of the earth like a wasteland. They are barely planted, barely sown, their stem hardly takes root in the ground when he blows on them and they wither, and a whirlwind carries them away like stubble.
>
> "To whom will you compare me, or who is my equal?" asks the Holy One. Look up and see! Who created these? He brings out the stars by number; he calls all of them by name. Because of his great power and strength, *not one of them is missing.*" (40:21–26, emphasis added)

Isaiah told the exiles, holding their unfulfilled desires and fear regarding their future, to use their senses.

He first said, *Look around. What do you see?* They can see the heavens. They can see the stars. What does looking at and thinking about creation do? Truths about the invisible God are seen in his visible creation, namely his eternal power and divine nature.[1] So when Isaiah told the exiles to look at the stars, he's again using scale and size. The number of stars overwhelms us. We still today cannot count them. But Isaiah tells us that God created each one and knows each one by name. *Not one is missing.*

Second, he told them to listen. *Have you not heard?* He called them to reference the stories they've heard from their ancestors about God's faithfulness and the work he'd done on their behalf. *Not one promise is missing.*

Isaiah seemingly said, *Think about this! Think about what you're hearing and seeing! Go outside and look at the stars! Listen to the truths people have told you about the trustworthiness of God!*

Isaiah attempted to call them out of their numbness, reminding them that God was with his people and working even at that moment to bring their deliverance and redemption to fruition. *God can be trusted, so do not fear!*

This is instructive for us as we ask our own hard questions and face an uncertain future. *What if we stay stuck here forever?*

The problem isn't that we face worries or questions; the problem comes when we choose to turn in the wrong direction to deal with those worries and questions.

We must not turn toward idols who eventually make us blind and unhearing and prideful and foolish. We must not put our

---

1. Romans 1:20.

hope in circumstances changing because that only makes God appear small and untrustworthy. We must not put our hope in ourselves by trying to control life and make it do what we want it to do, and then when it takes a left turn, we think God is uncaring and untrustworthy. We must not put our hope in other people, thinking they can rescue us or save us or give us significance, and then when they fail us or we fail them, we are devastated.

When we look at these things for our hope, we're looking for these things to give us what they cannot give. We must turn instead and see that God is all-knowing, all-powerful, and all-loving, all at the same time. No one can compare to him.

This is the idea Isaiah was trying to get at. He preached to a ragtag bunch of broken-down, seemingly forgotten exiles, who were wondering if God would keep his promises. Isaiah couldn't emphasize to them enough that God is able, God is engaged, and—this is important—*God is willing.*

You who feel forgotten and unseen, even buried, hear this:

> Jacob, why do you say, and Israel, why do you assert, "My way is hidden from the LORD, and my claim is ignored by my God"? Do you not know? Have you not heard? The LORD is the everlasting God, the Creator of the whole earth. He never becomes faint or weary; there is no limit to his understanding. He gives strength to the faint and strengthens the powerless. Youths may become faint and weary, and young men stumble and fall, but those who trust in the LORD will renew their strength; they will soar on wings like eagles;

they will run and not become weary, they will
walk and not faint. (Isa. 40:27–31)

God is not forgetful or tired. He is always working, never
sleeping. He understands every detail of your situation and knows
how to handle it perfectly. You are not hidden or ignored, and you
never will be.

What Isaiah proclaimed, remember, was a foretelling of the
future. In other words, when the exiles heard these words, God
hadn't delivered them yet. But we can't get around the emphasis
of Isaiah 40: *he will do it.*

And so they are called by Isaiah to be faithful waiters. Those
who waited on the Lord were promised strength and power in
uncertain times and circumstances. Theirs was a hope that certainly strengthened and fueled them as they faced life in exile.

Lessons Learned in the Waiting

As I said before, God made clear to me: I was to wait. I didn't
know what I was waiting for necessarily, and, as a compulsive
doer, waiting is not instinctive, nor is it easy. But in waiting, I
discovered many truths about God and myself that sustained me
and eventually transformed me.

The first truth I discovered was that my painful circumstances
were an important part of preparing the way for God's deliverance because they gave me clarity as to what felt off in my life and
what I specifically desired instead. For example, certain dynamics
in relationships I had come to accept as normal—even though
they didn't feel good to me—I saw with clarity and resolved to no
longer entertain.

The second truth I discovered in the waiting period was that my purpose and pursuit can never be about visibility for visibility's sake. If I pursue being seen so that others will applaud me, I will never be satisfied because it's self-idolatry. In other words, I needed to be careful not to swing from being unseen to the complete other side of *fighting* to be seen in order to protect myself from ever being unseen again.

The third truth is what I learned from Isaiah 40: look and listen.

Look for his deliverance. "I will keep watch for you, my strength, because God is my stronghold" (Ps. 59:9). When we're hurting, it's tempting to focus on the pain when instead we must look for how God is moving and working. Take solace in knowing he did not and will not capitulate to a person or circumstance or a wrong done against you. Recount his deeds; keep a written record you can refer to when you're struggling.

Listen to the old stories. When was he faithful to his promises? It's easy to focus on what we want God to do specifically for us, but what has he actually promised to do? What promises has he already fulfilled for you? Rehearse them repeatedly.

Here's a specific one to know and rehearse: everything God promised he would do for the exiles, he did.

Jeremiah prophesied that Judah's exile to Babylon would last seventy years. Persia conquered Babylon during Judah's exile, and Cyrus, king of Persia, whom the Bible says was "roused"[2] by the Lord himself, issued a proclamation that not only allowed the Jews to return home but summoned their neighbors to give them silver, gold, and livestock to help them get there.

---

2. Ezra 1:1.

What?!

God used a pagan nation and a pagan king to fulfill his promise to his people. The people left slavery not just with essentials but with riches! And of course the exile was seventy years long, just as Jeremiah prophesied. Who could have drawn up that specific plan? Who could have caused it to happen just as it was foretold?

Only our incomparable God.

If he can do that, he can deliver you, too.

Wait on him.

For Further Reflection

1. Have you experienced a situation where God acted in a confusing or disorienting way? What did you learn through that?

2. Have you experienced unseenness through self-disregard? How does knowing God created you, sees you, loves you, and has gifted you speak to your self-disregard?

3. Consider the questions Isaiah 40 draws out: Do you think your circumstances are too big or too complex for God? Do you think God doesn't have wisdom and knowledge enough to know exactly what you need? Do you think God doesn't have authority over everything and everyone affecting you? What about God's self-description in Isaiah 40 stands out to you and rebuts areas of fear or dread you have regarding your future?

Chapter 9

HE SEES SO HE ADVOCATES

I n the pain of my unseenness, one of the most persistent and anguished questions I scribbled in my prayer journal and spoke toward the sky was, "God, do you see what is happening to me?" Because I could see it all in vivid color.

In the aftermath of wounds inflicted by others, I'd begun replaying countless situations in my mind, watching scenes of my life as if I were sitting alone in a dark movie theater of my youth, the film projector whirring and the film reel flapping as the movie concluded. The scenes replaying in my mind were so detailed that I could practically look up and see the specks of dust finding the light of the projector.

I watched scenes where my concerns had been dismissed. Having been proven right about those concerns, I then turned to witness the fallout of those concerns becoming reality, most of its consequences landing on me. I watched scenes where I'd been required to absorb my own hurt feelings to protect or save another's feelings. I observed myself in relational situation after relational situation where rather than being advocated for, I was silenced, ignored, and left to fend for myself.

I couldn't believe what I was watching. Although I'd sensed for a while that something was off, I had not known, nor had I seen. Even then, watching the movie back, I tried to convince myself this wasn't my actual life, attempting to mentally surface evidence to prove how loved, seen, and protected I actually was. I had such a good life! And I was so independent and strong! Everyone had said so (albeit it with a slight eye roll) since I was young!

But for the first time, I was honest with myself. The truth was that I *was* buried. The truth was that it didn't much matter to certain people what I felt or wanted or needed. The truth was that no one was going to pull me out of the shadows and advocate for me. The truth was I'd repeatedly allowed this behavior.

And I was done; I was no longer willing to absorb these things or leave them unchallenged.

I then had a sense of who was running the film projector and why I'd found myself alone in the theater, tears of shock running down my face.

God was showing me these scenes. Not only did he see what was happening, but he wanted *me* to see it, too—to stare into reality and become so uncomfortable with what I saw that it would enact changes inside of me and, subsequently, in my relationships. Reality was so heavy and blinding that, through it, God would eventually offer multiple people an opportunity to watch the replaying scenes and see how they'd intentionally or unintentionally played a role in my pain. Some people made the most of that opportunity through deep repentance and lasting change;

others chose to remain in their delusion, unwilling to acknowledge reality.

In every scene, God's presence loomed large, and in this I took great comfort. I kept asking, "God, do you see what's happening to me?," and he made clear he not only saw but he'd seen it before I could. What was happening to me wasn't sitting right with him, and he'd come to make it right.

I'd despaired, thinking no one could or would pull me out of the shadows, but he stood by my side, whispering, *I see what is happening, and I will advocate for you.*

He Sees How You've Been Sinned Against

Where do you need an advocate? Are there areas of your life that feel hidden from view? Have you spoken up for yourself only to be dismissed? Have wounds been inflicted that others won't acknowledge or apologize for? Are you being asked to absorb what is not yours to absorb? Does it seem your "wounder" has gotten away with little consequence?

We find ourselves now exploring the realm of injustice, a category of unseenness that is especially vexing because it is, by its nature, an unresolved experience. Injustice occurs when a wrong has been done and hasn't been named, righted, or reconciled. For many who experience it, injustice is ongoing, and for some it is lifelong. It can come in the form of an unsolved crime, the color of one's skin being consistently degraded, a family secret, spiritual abuse, or any number of experiences that birth agony, rage, shame, and confusion in us.

For me, my friend's unwillingness to acknowledge how she had deeply hurt me left me alone in what should have been a two-person process of reconciliation and, if possible, restoration, which exacerbated my sense of injustice. I just wanted her to acknowledge reality, and it felt unjust that she couldn't or wouldn't agree with me on what seemed so obvious.

Where there is injustice, advocacy is needed: someone to step in and speak up, to listen and believe, to protect and defend, and ultimately to make wrong things right.

How fitting, then, that one of Jesus's names is Advocate.

Because our first and most basic need as a human being is justice with God—our wrongs being made right so we can be in relationship with a right and holy God. First John 2:1 practically sings a song into the weary and irretrievably broken sinner's soul: "My little children, I am writing you these things so that you may not sin. But if anyone does sin, we have an advocate with the Father—Jesus Christ the righteous one."

At the cross and through the grave, Jesus stepped in and spoke up to the Father for us, taking on himself the righteous wrath of God for our sin. He made all your wrongs right by becoming the wrong for you.[1]

But God's advocacy for you goes beyond your own sin. Jesus acts as your advocate when your enemy shouts words of shame and guilt. He protects and defends you when temptation comes your way. He not only receives your confession but promises to cleanse and transform you into his image. And one last thing: Jesus advocates for justice when others sin against you.

In Jesus's work on the cross, forgiveness for sin is available to anyone who receives it by faith. We need his work because our sin has offset the scales of justice; we have sinned against a holy

---

1. 2 Corinthians 5:21.

God. Jesus's death and resurrection, then, reset the scales of justice, making us righteous before God—something we ourselves cannot do.

But the cross also boldly declares that *all* sin must be accounted for. No sin has or ever will be swept under the rug, ignored, or allowed by God. We have a God Who Sees, and included in his scope of seeing is the sinful harm that's been done to you. When he sees that harm, by the nature of his justness, he pursues justice on your behalf in the perfect time and in the perfect way.

Peek into Luke 7:36–50 with me to observe Jesus's advocacy of justice for one particular woman: "Then one of the Pharisees invited [Jesus] to eat with him. [Jesus] entered the Pharisee's house and reclined at the table. And a woman in the town who was a sinner found out that Jesus was reclining at the table in the Pharisee's house. She brought an alabaster jar of perfume and stood behind him at his feet, weeping, and began to wash his feet with her tears. She wiped his feet with her hair, kissing them and anointing them with the perfume" (vv. 36–38).

Let's stop and consider this woman. She is not identified by her name but only as "a sinner." Her actions imply she wouldn't refute this identifier. She knows the depth of her sin, which is always necessary before one can begin to comprehend the height and depth and width of God's grace. Her courageous vulnerability in a room full of men who seem to know her backstory almost takes one's breath away. This is a woman who *knows* she is seen by Jesus and knows all her many wrongs have been made right.

But that doesn't necessarily translate to others seeing her or treating her with dignity:

When the Pharisee who had invited [Jesus] saw this, he said to himself, "This man, if he were a prophet, would know who and what kind of woman this is who is touching him—she's a sinner!"

Jesus replied to him, "Simon, I have something to say to you."

He said, "Say it, teacher."

"A creditor had two debtors. One owed five hundred denarii, and the other fifty. Since they could not pay it back, he graciously forgave them both. So, which of them will love him more?"

Simon answered, "I suppose the one he forgave more."

"You have judged correctly," he told him. (vv. 39–43)

Notice that the Pharisee doesn't verbalize what's in his heart, but Jesus knows it anyway. The Pharisee never verbally or physically harmed the woman, but his dismissive *thoughts* were enough for Jesus to step in and correct the man.

He not only corrected the man, calling wrong things wrong and making wrong things right, but Jesus invited him to see the woman rightly:

Turning to the woman, he said to Simon, "Do you see this woman? I entered your house; you gave me no water for my feet, but she, with her tears, has washed my feet and wiped them with her hair. You gave me no kiss, but she hasn't

stopped kissing my feet since I came in. You
didn't anoint my head with olive oil, but she has
anointed my feet with perfume. Therefore I tell
you, her many sins have been forgiven; that's
why she loved much. But the one who is forgiven
little, loves little." Then he said to her, "Your sins
are forgiven."

Those who were at the table with him began
to say among themselves, "Who is this man who
even forgives sins?"

And he said to the woman, "Your faith has
saved you. Go in peace." (vv. 44–50)

Jesus would not allow the woman to be harmed by sinful,
unseeing men. He publicly commended her humility, gratefulness, and repentance and sent her off in peace with a new identifier: *forgiven*.

He made wrong things right, not just for the woman but also
for those who dismissed and disregarded her.

He advocated for her.

Temptations When There Isn't Resolution

Complete healing (and appropriate corrective action) from
unseenness requires a *resolute* belief that we have an advocate in
Jesus Christ and a just judge in God the Father because, when
we've been wounded and we can't bring it to resolution, the temptations are legion.

In the face of injustice, we may be tempted to overcorrect
and become a right-fighter who loses track of our own propensity

to sin and, thus, our own need for the gracious forgiveness Jesus offers.

We may be tempted to doubt God will ever make right what remains wrong and instead take matters into our own hands, meting out punishment or retaliation, in effect placing ourselves in God's judgment seat.

We may be tempted toward hopelessness, unable to take appropriate corrective action or, when necessary, to lovingly confront those who have sinned against us.

If we believe he stood idly by while sin grew in the dark, we may even develop anger or distrust toward God.

I can name each of these temptations because, in the face of unseenness, I've given into them all. I've had difficulty letting details fade into the background; I've experienced temptation as an almost compulsive need to remember and recall the specifics of others' sin. I'm afraid I'll be hurt in similar ways again, so I must be on guard. My speech has been laced with bitterness and cynicism. Therein each of these responses lies the stench of unforgiveness and distrust of God's all-seeing eye and his justice.

But I'm convinced God was convicting others of their sin against me, even though they were unwilling to heed him. I came to this conclusion as I invited trusted loved ones to watch the replaying scenes of my story with me and discovered in their responses that God had been speaking to them about me in ways they'd ignored. They were grieved at how they turned away from his conviction.

I also thought about close friends who had expressed gentle concern along the way, pressing on a reality I hadn't wanted to see at the time. God had been attempting to speak to me through them.

In both ways—attempting to convict others and convict myself—he'd advocated for me, far before I knew I needed it.

For each of us, however, certain things are unresolved and will likely remain that way. I've lived long enough to know that truth always rises out of the shadows into the light, even when it's been buried so long that everyone but the wounded forgets it happened. Scripture says this will be true for every wrong in the end: "I tell you that on the day of judgment people will have to account for every careless word they speak" (Matt. 12:36). And if every careless word will be accounted for, certainly every careless action will be as well. Each sin will be accounted for: named, acknowledged as sin by the perfect arbiter of right and wrong, and dealt with perfectly—forgiven if the person is in Christ, added to the debt ledger if not.

Truth will rise, but in the meantime, as I hold fast to the truth that God sees and advocates, I find things in my own heart that need changing, and I am the only one I can change. One such discovery: my desire for redemption of injustice is right and good because it mirrors God's desire, but the *means* of redemption I want are often far removed from the means God uses.

I want immediate vindication; God's redemption of injustice typically involves an uncomfortable amount of time.

I want his advocacy because I want to be right and proven right; God's redemption of injustice asks me more often to consider myself and my own need for his transformation.

I want to be seen according to my own definition of seenness: never again tucked away, never again overlooked, never again asked to sit in silence or in the shadows. God's redemption of injustice reminds me that there are things only he can see and know, and this is good.

God's true advocacy means that *he* is vindicated, found right, seen and, therefore, worshipped and adored. *He* is the hero of true justice, where what is right and good and beautiful and pure wins out in the end.

So in one breath I may ask, "God, do you see what is happening to me?" But in the next, I must step down from the judge's seat, surrendering instead to perfect wisdom, timing, conviction, and judgment. I must trust that God will not let anyone remain in their blindness, delusion, and dysfunction if they are willing to be rescued from it. I must not let my own delusion grow through unforgiveness and self-righteous anger. I must not, in response to being unseen, allow my own hardness of heart to cause me to become unseeing in relation to others—for example, being unwilling to consider how God can forgive those who have acted unjustly against me.

There is no settled soul living in the land of self-righteous anger and self-determined justice.

Knowing Jesus advocates for me has been the biggest help and most steady comfort as I've navigated the bumpy terrain of knowing how to respond to my personal heartache and to those who contributed to it.

I can release it all to him, knowing he saw it all, knowing he makes wrong things right in the perfect way and in his perfect timing. If I get involved, trying to make things right on my own, I will only mess it up further.

Releasing it to Jesus, my advocate, has allowed me to focus on outcomes for myself like a growing intimacy with God and healthy relationships with the most important people in my life. And that's exactly what's happened. Pouring out my complaints to God, asking him to act according to his justice, restraining myself from my most fleshly, retaliatory responses by trusting in him instead—all of these have contributed to a healthy emotional connection with him. And in my human relationships, I have been given clarity about patterns of relational dysfunction (some that I contributed to) and pathways forward for growth.

In other words, Jesus carries the weight of the problems and consequences of injustice and the responsibility for making justice happen. I carry the weight of obedience. *Yes, Lord, make all things right. And in the process, let me live rightly. Let me not add to the injustice. Let me live in your deliverance.*

Friend, God has seen it all. Release the consequences and outcomes to him. Release the person who hurt you to him. Release the demanding compulsion for vengeance or vindication.

You have an Advocate. Let him go to work on your behalf.

> Do not be agitated by evildoers;
>   do not envy those who do wrong.
> For they wither quickly like grass
>   and wilt like tender green plants.
>
> Trust in the LORD and do what is good;
>   dwell in the land and live securely.
> Take delight in the LORD,
>   and he will give you your heart's desires.
> Commit your way to the LORD;
>   trust in him, and he will act,
>   making your righteousness shine like the dawn,
>   your justice like the noonday.

Be silent before the LORD and wait expectantly
    for him;
do not be agitated by one who prospers in his
    way,
by the person who carries out evil plans.

Refrain from anger and give up your rage;
do not be agitated—it can only bring harm.
For evildoers will be destroyed,
but those who put their hope in the LORD
will inherit the land.

For the LORD loves justice
and will not abandon his faithful ones.
They are kept safe forever,
but the children of the wicked will be destroyed.
    (Ps. 37:1–9, 28)

The Outcome We Want

When we step back and wait on the Lord, we eventually discover that he's an incredible Redeemer. God is like an artist who
combines recycled materials to make something beautiful and
entirely different from what he started with.

Hagar named him the God Who Sees. I name him Recycler.

I've discovered this about him as I continually release my pain
to the Lord and, as a by-product, release my debtors from what
their sin has cost me.

When we're living with injustice, forgiveness is not easy.
Forgiveness can sometimes feel like a finish line at the end of a
long race that keeps moving out ahead of us: we think we're finally

there; and, nope, even a passing remembrance hits, and we realize how much more pavement there is for our feet to travel.

That's why Joseph's story in Scripture has been so meaningful to me. I've scoured the pages of Genesis for details on how he forgave several life-changing injustices done against him.

His brothers sold him into slavery to a traveling band of Egyptians. He was purchased by a political leader, whose wife sold him up the river because Joseph refused her seduction. As a result, he was sentenced to prison, where he helped a man get released who promptly forgot about him, leaving him to languish.

Joseph must have done much soul-searching in his prison cell because one day he got out of prison (thanks to God). He rose in the ranks under that political leader to become his right-hand man (thanks to God). And one day Joseph's brothers appeared before him (not knowing it was him) in great need. On that day, Joseph was ready (thanks to God). Ready to forgive, ready with kindness and affection, ready to serve those the rest of us might label his enemies.

Let me show you Joseph's words that I've clung to, a lifeline as I have run toward forgiveness. They were his first words to his brothers when he announced to them who he was. Here they are in summary form. (You can read Joseph's words in context, starting in Genesis 45):

> *You sold me here.*
> *God sent me before you.*
> *God sent me before you for you.*
> *It was not you who sent me here but God.*

Joseph acknowledged reality: he was unjustly sinned against. That wasn't OK with him or with God. But Joseph had also seen over many years how God had turned their sin against him into something good, which enabled him to extend kindness and forgiveness toward his brothers. He said it three times, almost with a sense of urgency that they hear and understand: *God sent me here. God took your sin against me and flipped it on its head, giving me good instead.* He even took it one step further: *God didn't just do this for me. He did this for you, too.* Joseph provided for his brothers out of the good that had come through the bad, from their hands!

Everything evil done against Joseph was recycled for good, and the good and evil were not in equal portions. On the scale, good far outweighed the evil, and the good was not just for Joseph. It was for the benefit of a whole nation, *including his brothers.*

In Genesis 50, the brothers finally acknowledged their sin against Joseph. But we discover he had already released them into God's hands long before, refusing to sit on the judgment seat: "Am I in the place of God?" (v. 19). Joseph's kindness to them led to their repentance.

Forgiveness is a long process, but somewhere on the path, I was able to look back and see a "flipping" had started to happen. Miraculously, I could see what Joseph saw. God had brought so much good from something so painful that I began to thank him for the bad as catalyst for the good.

Yes, you read that right.

I began thanking him for what hurt me because he'd used what hurt me to heal me.

He recycled what was meant for evil, and what I thought might kill me, into something that is good and full of life.

The God Who Sees is the God who recycles.

And he wants to recycle your pain into something beautiful.

For Further Reflection

1. How does considering the cross not only regarding your sin but regarding the sin of those who have wounded you affect how you consider your situation?

2. Are you experiencing any of the temptations mentioned in this chapter in the midst of your own injustice or an unresolved situation? If so, which ones? What truth about God or the way he acts helps you combat that temptation?

3. As you ask, "God, do you see what is happening to me?," you can call on God to act according to his attributes. Read Psalm 94, an imprecatory psalm—a plea for God to act justly. What requests does the psalmist make as he faces injustice? What requests do you need to make of God in the face of your unresolved situation?

Chapter 10

HE SEES AND IS PLEASED

As I clawed and crawled my way out of the desert of unseen-ness with fresh wounds and fresh vision alike, I remember saying to my husband on particularly difficult "wrestling" days, "No one will ever know what I've endured and how hard I've fought to forgive."

I had not kept my struggle from those who could handle the weight of my suffering, and dear friends had willingly entered into the fray—each one a sure and steady balm for my soul. But my specific experiences occurred in a larger context that at times felt like living in a soundproof room: few outside my confines could hear me when I screamed in frustration or when I cried tears in pain, and as far as I could tell, I mostly still lived outside of the view of others. Out of sight (out of sound?), out of mind.

That larger context to which I'm referring?

Vocational ministry.

I was then and still am a pastor's wife, and when studies repeat-edly describe the pastor's wife as one of the loneliest women in the church, I think they are hinting at the disorienting experience of living in a soundproof room. It's not that the pastor's wife doesn't try to escape her confines by being as human as possible and, as everyone tells her to be, herself. It's not that she doesn't reach out for help when she needs it or that she doesn't pursue friendship and connection. And it's not that she doesn't fight to embrace the context in which God has placed her, constantly beating back cynicism, discouragement, and bitterness in order to maintain her joy. It's just that few people know what to do when the pastor's wife falls apart at the heart seams or, in more mundane times, merely has a bad day and a few needs of her own.

There was a moment in my unseenness when I realized that, just as any hurting Christian does, I desperately needed the care of Christ's body. I needed a listening ear, wise counsel, prayer, understanding, and, like a cup of cold water in the desert, a kind word. But because I was married to the leader of all these people, I did not actually have what others have: a pastor. Yes, my husband is my pastor, but there are times and seasons when one's husband cannot also be one's pastor, and I was drowning in just such a time and season.

I sought help outside our church, but I wanted so badly to be seen and cared for by those inside my church. They are, every single one, lovely, godly people with good intentions, and it's possible I didn't communicate well enough or often enough with the right people. But those who were standing the closest seemed so frightened that their pastor and his wife might not be infallible after all.

To me, the tepid response was another blow, a gut punch when I was already suffering from a broken spirit.

I found myself pulling back, making needed space for myself, but also unsure, shaken, and extremely self-protective.

In our decades-long ministry life, I'd learned long before how to serve in "secret" or unrecognized by others, and how serving in secret, so that one hand gives and the other hand doesn't even know about it, is the most fulfilling way to serve.[1] Of course, I learned that secret joy of secret service when my ministry to others went unacknowledged and unappreciated, resulting in a heart swollen and diseased with indignation and entitlement. The Lord has not failed to use every such moment of feeling unappreciated or taken for granted to refine my motives and excise selfishness and a desire for self-glory.

I'd even learned to suffer in secret. I don't mean that I haven't shared my struggles with others, but I do mean that as a ministry leader, some things would be inappropriate to ask those we serve to carry with us or enter into. Some suffering or struggle must be kept out of view to guard the health of the church and the health of all involved.

But to receive gaping wounds from those you're called by God to serve is a secret suffering that is difficult to navigate. No one will ever know the things that have been said or left unsaid. No one will know the cost of absorbing what's been absorbed. No one will ever know the forgiveness that's been offered or, for that matter, the details of how God has comforted and healed.

Some aspects of the Christian life happen in secret places, between God and his beloved alone. It could be characterized, perhaps, as a secret sanctification and a secret obedience.

---

1. Matthew 6:3.

But when I found myself saying to Kyle, "No one will ever know what I've endured and how hard I've fought to forgive," it was marked by acidity and grumbling. My self-righteousness and pride wanted others to know and applaud me. In a sense, it was a question to God: "Does it even matter what I'm doing for you, God?"

Kyle knew as much as another human being could possibly know about my experience without climbing into my skin, hearing the jumble of thoughts rattling around in my brain, and feeling the beat of my heart. As much as he wanted to, he knew he couldn't know every crevice and corner, so he simply nodded, letting me know he was listening, letting me talk it out.

I knew, however, that he'd recognized the edge in my voice.

He waited, inviting the silence to settle between us.

"But God sees," he said, gently, quietly. "And he knows."

Why did that somehow not seem enough?

Reward for Secret Service

You may not be in vocational ministry like me, but serving in vocational ministry or being a pastor's wife is not the only context in which we may experience the specific category of unseenness we've labeled a lack of appreciation: feeling that those who receive benefit from our service don't understand what it's costing us or do not acknowledge the benefit they've received from it.

The larger context in which you may navigate this type of unseenness may be motherhood, singleness, marriage, a job, volunteer work, friendship, family relationships, church, or any number of other things.

You may be frustrated because you feel taken for granted, overlooked for promotion, or like another cog in a big wheel that may or may not be noticed if you disappeared.

Consider the source of your frustration or discouragement. Might your feelings be legitimate? Absolutely. We know well how easy it is to view people, as my husband often says, as scenery or machinery, and when we realize we're the scenery or machinery in someone else's life, it's hurtful, especially when it occurs within our closest or most important relationships.

I've discovered over the years that my context, soundproof room and all, has also been the greenhouse in which God has grown my faith. In other words, when I consider the source of my frustration regarding a lack of appreciation, and when I find myself thinking that somehow it's not enough that God sees all that I do in his name for others, there is something sinister growing in the soil of my heart. My motivations are askew.

I look back now over decades of service and recognize that God has intentionally withheld appreciation from others at the times I was most desperate for it. He did this not to be a withholding Father but because he loved me enough to keep me from what wouldn't have been good for me. In the greenhouse, he weeded my heart of the compulsion to ensure people know what I've done, how I've sacrificed, and how I've helped—what would've eventually choked out the good seed of God's grace in my life. Now, anytime I find myself getting angry or put off when others obviously don't understand what I've sacrificed, I remember I'm in a greenhouse where faith is grown, and I return in my mind to a specific passage of Scripture:

> Be careful not to practice your righteousness in
> front of others to be seen by them. Otherwise,
> you have no reward with your Father in heaven.
> So whenever you give to the poor, don't sound a
> trumpet before you, as the hypocrites do in the
> synagogues and on the streets, to be applauded
> by people. Truly I tell you, they have their reward.
> But when you give to the poor, don't let your left
> hand know what your right hand is doing, so that
> your giving may be in secret. And your Father
> who sees in secret will reward you. (Matt. 6:1–4)

I remember, through this verse, that God may keep others from expressing appreciation not just to keep me from something that's not good for me but also because he wants to give me something better: his lasting pleasure and his eternal reward rather than the passing burst of applause from others that acts like cotton candy in the mouth—sweet at first but lacking substance, leaving me empty and craving more.

I also remember that Jesus makes a distinction between things practiced for public consumption and those same things practiced for God's pleasure. One is a dead end, and one bears fruit.

There is a reward for those who offer secret service to God from a place of private devotion. What is that reward? One day, when we stand face-to-face with Jesus, we will get to hear the sweetest words possible as the summary of our life: "Well done, good and faithful servant."[2] Rather than a generic statement or a rubber-stamp statement, he will say this with specifics in mind:

---

2. Matthew 25:23.

"And whoever gives even a cup of cold water to one of these little ones because he is a disciple, truly I tell you, he will never lose his reward" (Matt. 10:42).

Jesus sees you repeatedly wipe that bottom in his name, and he sees you stay late to clean up for his eyes only, and he sees how you set aside your agenda to sit with that hurting person because of him. For these things, he says, you will be rewarded with a reward you can't lose. Jesus doesn't hand out cotton-candy rewards.

But rewards aren't just saved for later; there is a secret reward *now*, too—a joy we cannot birth, no matter the amount of labor.

Jesus said it is more blessed to give to others than to receive.[3] I find this statement interesting because it's just that: a statement, not a command. He seems to be conveying to us that life and relationships will be better, more satisfying, and more joyful for us if we focus not on what people are doing for us but on what we can do for them.

Proverbs 11:25 (ESV) says it like this: "Whoever brings blessing will be enriched, and one who waters will himself be watered."

Scripture indicates that putting more emphasis on giving "waters" us in some way. I used to read that verse and think that if I served others, they would serve me or thank me in return. I now read this verse from the context of my greenhouse and see that, instead, it means we enjoy a *specific happiness* reserved for those who serve in Jesus's name. Isn't there a satisfaction we feel when we're able to meet a need or give an encouraging word? That's the watering Proverbs talks about—the joy of being used by God. And that's the specific happiness of serving.

---

3. Acts 20:35.

Loving and serving others in the name of Christ and for his eyes only triples the joy: our service is for the blessing of the one we serve, it is a fragrant and pleasing aroma to God, and it produces in us the unique joy of having been a vessel to share Christ's love.

And so, when I prepare to serve someone or I find myself grumbling in an act of service, I simply say out loud, "This is for you, Jesus. Do with this what you will."

No expectations. No trying to control the outcomes. No thought of what others might think or say. I'm giving up a desire for validation or celebration. No matter if there are hundreds of women in the room with me, *it's just you and me here, Jesus. May I serve you alone, and may you get the honor and praise.*

Service is not valid only if it's acknowledged and appreciated by the one served. Service is valid when it's done in love and faith, in honor of Christ.

And he always acknowledges it. Always.

Internal Service to God

But God sees more than our service to others. He also sees our hearts. In other words, he sees what we do externally in his name, but he also sees what we do *internally* in his name. One of my favorite verses captures this truth: "For God is not unjust; he will not forget your work and *the love* you demonstrated for his name by serving the saints—and by continuing to serve them" (Heb. 6:10, emphasis added).

While it's often difficult to serve others with the right motivations, I daresay the hardest acts of service are the internal acts: willfully carrying another's emotional burden; deciding to forgive and, in effect, release the debt another owes us; choosing to love those who have not chosen to love us; refusing to retaliate or seek or our own vindication; or protecting someone who did not protect us.

The hardest work I've ever done internally is forgiving the one who, thus far, has refused to acknowledge hurting me so deeply. I've spent countless hours having conversations in my head because, despite several attempts, I know I can't have the actual conversation. The rupture will likely not be repaired.

Once again, *it's just you and me here, Jesus.*

Why is this type of secret service in Jesus's name so much harder? Because there is no chance of a pat on the back or a word of appreciation. It is *truly* secret; no one can ever possibly see into our heart except for One.

We tend to overvalue appreciation for what people can see and undervalue what they can't, but I wonder what is most important to Jesus.

In this private work of forgiveness, I find some motivation in the idea that forgiveness is what's good for me and for my own well-being, but that has only taken me so far. The only motivation that has continually moved me forward is looking at myself in light of Jesus and Jesus in light of me. In fact, in this private ongoing act of forgiveness, I've thought more than ever about Jesus and his forgiveness of me and have simply marveled. As I began this process, I wrote this in my journal as a reflection on Isaiah 53 and Good Friday:

> We thought he wasn't worth esteem. He wasn't charismatic, good-looking, or powerful enough. When we looked at him through human eyes,

he left much to be desired. "What does he have
to offer?" we said, shrugging and yawning.
Certainly, nothing we were looking for.

In fact, he repulsed us. He was an outsider,
a misfit, easy to disregard. He was too much
to handle—a magnet for grief, pain, sorrow,
weakness—all the things (and all the people carrying them) we avoid and ignore.

And so we looked away.

But, in fact, he deserved the greatest esteem
that could be given—the whole world's combined. For while we looked away, snickering at
him, chasing our own esteem, he willfully took
on the consequences of our rejection. When we
disregarded him, he regarded us. When we dis-
esteemed him, he esteemed us. Not only did he
take the consequences of our pride, greed, lust,
and self-glory, but he took on the personal pain
of our rejection—a severe injustice. He didn't
deserve us, nor did we deserve him.

Though he had every right to claim righteous anger, he didn't throw reality in our faces,
demanding our esteem, demanding we acknowledge his worth. Rather, he took our disregard
patiently, intentionally, lovingly, and meekly,
because he had our good, our healing, our joy,
our salvation in mind. While we considered
him cursed and spit our curses upon him, he

considered how he could win for us the approval
he knew so well: the approval of the Father.

By his wounds—the pain we ourselves
inflicted—we are healed. How can it be? How
does he do it, this forgiveness?

I think I know how. He wanted to please his Father. And
because he obeyed, absorbing more than we can possibly understand or imagine, God now sees us and is pleased.

This is enough to see me through.

We may not have esteemed him correctly then, but we can
now. We can live our lives in honor of him: absorbing pain
inflicted upon us by choosing forgiveness, giving mercy when we
want to hate, giving up our rights for the sake of love instead of
fighting for them, regarding and esteeming others when they dis-
honor us, and receiving the gift of peace Christ died to earn us.

We love because he first loved us.

We forgive because he first forgave us.

We serve him because he first served us.

Remember, our service is not valid only if it's acknowledged
and appreciated by the one served. Service is valid when it's done
in love and faith, in honor of Christ.

He always acknowledges. Always.

He sees, and he is pleased.

For Further Reflection

1. In what circumstances are you asking, "Does it matter what I
do for you, God?"

2. Does it sometimes not seem "enough" that God sees and knows what you do in his name? Why do you think that is?

3. Have you experienced a time when God seemed to withhold praise or appreciation from people in order to reveal your heart to you? And to give you something better? How is God's praise better?

4. Have you considered that God sees the internal work you do in his name? How does considering that he sees your heart help you press on in difficult things, like forgiveness?

Part Five

RESTORED VISION

Chapter 11

SEEING WITH NEW EYES

N ear the city where we church-planted, there is an old, abandoned train tunnel, built in the 1850s, that in recent years was refurbished and reopened as part of a biking and walk-ing path. The train tunnel itself is almost a mile long and cuts through the base of a mountain, so traversing the path safely from end to end necessitates a headlamp or flashlight.

When Kyle and I took our boys through the tunnel for the first time, we entered on one side, expecting darkness to immedi-ately wash over us. Instead, we walked for a while to the light of the sun at our backs, marveling at the old stones we could see in detail that formed the tunnel wall, water dripping down from the mountain on its curved sides. But eventually we reached a point in our journey where we could not see the light from the opening behind us. We switched on our headlamps and phone flashlights, but the artificial light lit up only a small section in front of us. I strained to see the opening I'd been promised was ahead, but I couldn't see any hint of sunlight. A sense of panic and fear washed over me, as did the cool air and the realization that I was half a mile from both the exit behind me and the exit before me.

In the suffocating darkness, I longed for the piercing, clarifying light of day, but all I could do was take one more step toward the promise of light.

Going through a really long season of unseenness was like going through that tunnel, except the "me" that entered the darkness is not the same "me" that came out on the other side. And that is good. Unseenness has marked me, but it has also changed me in ways I didn't know I needed.

God has given me new vision, not lit by artificial, self-made light but lit up by the light of the noonday sun. I return often to Psalm 36:9, for it describes what I've experienced: "For the wellspring of life is with you. By means of your light we see light."

I feel as if I entered a tunnel by God's providence that kept getting darker and darker. Unable to locate the entrance or exit, I began to despair of the light, wondering in the deepest darkness if God saw and would act on my behalf. I asked him all my hard questions, and he patiently received them. Many times, however, my eyes struggling to focus in the dark, I desired immediate escape from the tunnel. Inevitably, a supernatural light flickered before me, illuminating the next step to take, consoling me when panic and fear surrounded me.

One day, the light I thought would never come appeared as a pinprick in the distance. With each step I took, the light grew bigger, and I could more easily orient myself to my surroundings. And then, there I was: exiting the tunnel on the other side, blinded by the light of day. Just as I'd taken in afresh the leaves on the trees and the specific blue of the sky when I'd exited the train tunnel, as I exited unseenness, I gulped the goodness of God with renewed vision and what I'd thought, in the deepest of darkness, might not ever return: renewed joy.

In the darkness, only guided by faith and the flickering fire of God's Word, I'd learned to see through his eyes. I saw him seeing me, and this seeing changed everything.

This is the work God does. He takes us through unseenness to show us something may need his careful, surgical attention. He did this work in me.

In your light do we see light.

When I walked out into the sun, having traversed the darkness of unseenness, not only had I been changed but I knew some things in my life needed to change as well.

Knowing (and believing) I was seen by God gave me a renewed vision regarding three aspects of my life: how I viewed myself, how I viewed others, and how I viewed my "middle of the tunnel" circumstances.

This "seeing" is available to you as well. You may have a sense that God is taking you into a season of darkness, but the light is still at your back. You may be in the deepest darkness of the tunnel, despairing that light will never return. Or you may see the pinprick of light ahead and simply need reassurance from a fellow traveler that it's not a mirage. No matter where your foot falls, in his light you will see light again. And you'll know you're drawing closer to his light when you also see what I've seen through his eyes.

In his light, we see our idolatry. I was so wounded by several people close to me—the impetus for entering the tunnel— that I was surprised to discover the internal workings of my own deluded heart revealed before me in the darkness.

At first, I admit, I did not want to see. But God persistently pointing to what he saw in my heart, and his insistence I give it careful attention was, I see now, his personal invitation to me to experience *true life*. Recall the first phrase of Psalm 36:9: "For the wellspring of life is with you."

Holding idolatry in our hearts cannot coexist with holding the wellspring of life—the peace, joy, and satisfaction Jesus offers. We must reject, repent of, and release what keeps us from the wellspring of life.

In some ways this means relaxing into rather than fighting the "hiddenness" of being Christ's. As Colossians 3:3 says, "For you died, and your life is hidden with Christ in God." But for those, like us, whose deepest wound is feeling unseen or disregarded, being "hidden" away in Christ can be extremely difficult to accept as enough. Something in us screams, "Never again!" The wound has birthed a fighter or a despair-er, and it acts as such a good shield against future hurt that we struggle to accept hiddenness as a good part of the Christian life.

When we feel "tucked away," how does knowing that our life is hidden in Christ give us profound soul rest? It helps to look at the futility and idolatry of ways we've sought seenness.

I'd sought vitality and purpose in things other than him, some in specific yet unconscious response to being unseen. Because my greatest wound in life was unseenness, visibility (or at least avoiding invisibility) had become overly important to me. My identity, in fact, hung too seriously on being visible and, in that visibility, being approved of.

A sense of seenness in order to feel secure, I recognized, could never again be my goal. And one way I've done that all my life—my fig-leaf strategy, as I mentioned previously—is to *do*, to take action. I'm a person who sees holes, problems, and opportunities and immediately sets out to fill, solve, and create. That's who I've been since I was a teenager, and it's worked for me for a long time in areas of life like church planting, parenting, and writing.

But suddenly my doing had stopped working. I found myself sprinting full speed into brick wall after brick wall. I saw holes and problems I couldn't fill and solve, no matter how hard I tried.

In other words, whatever agenda I set for myself, God thwarted. He allowed the brick walls. He walked me through the tunnel that I could not "agenda" myself out of. What I'd known to be so sure about myself, my relationships, and my calling began to fall apart.

However, in the darkness of the tunnel, God made me *more* sure of these things, but he's changed how I enact them. He's asked me to surrender my artificial, self-made flashlight I've used to make my own way, and instead he's required that I let him lead me with a pillar of fire. In his light, to see light. Not in my own light.

I'm still the same Christine who sees holes, problems, and opportunities and wants to fill, solve, and create. But the lesson in the confusion and pain of the tunnel was that the Lord is my Shepherd. Of course that truth was ingrained in me long ago, but I finally *experienced* it as truth, and that has made all the difference.

I am not meant to walk *with* the Lord; I am meant to *follow behind* him. Though he has created me with a go-getter personality, I'm not meant to run full speed ahead without him, emphasizing the gift above the Giver. I can't tell you how much I've done this very thing in my life and how much, in doing so, I've caused my own grief.

I see all this now, here on the other side of the tunnel.

One way I'm living as a follower is waiting on God. Remember, he had spoken that word—*wait?* He continued speaking it to me in countless moments along this path of suffering. *But, Lord, what do I do?* Wait. *But, Lord, when will this end?* Wait. *Lord, do you see?* Wait.

Waiting is not passive. It's the most active word in the Christian life because waiting is following. And doesn't the psalmist have something to say about what happens when we follow? "He lets me lie down in green pastures; he leads me beside quiet waters. He renews my life; he leads me along the right paths for his name's sake" (Ps. 23:2–3).

He is a good Shepherd. He will not make us visible for the sake of ourselves, but his seeing us makes us safe to be fully present with him. This is the goal to set our sights on: relational, emotional, and spiritual vitality, vulnerable to him, vulnerable with others, and tenderhearted toward the vulnerable around us.

In his light, we see his compassion for us. In addition to my fig-leaf strategy of compulsive doing, I'd spent my entire life berating myself for not doing or being enough. In other words, I learned to repeat to myself the messages I'd heard from others: that I was selfish for having preferences and desires, demanding for wanting relationships and circumstances to be different, overly emotional for having feelings, and singularly at fault for whatever was "off" in a relationship.

One who receives these messages learns to hide her true feelings, thoughts, and desires—most of all from herself.

God made us each individually who we are. He's seen the forces that have shaped us, including the situations or relationships in which we've been harmed. He doesn't overlook those moments or tell us to get over it. He is not impatient with our humanity. He does not berate his children. He is, instead, a safe refuge (Pss. 5:11–12; 31; 142), a welcoming presence for all of who we are—emotions, hurts, desires, fears, and all. He has compassion for us and longs for us to be who he's created us to be and live according to the unique gifts and skills he's given us. *This is an act of worship to God our Creator.*

When we have lived unseen, it is far easier to hide ourselves than to live our specific life for Christ. We fear critique and further dismissal.

The good news is that, because God sees, we don't have to fester in our wounds or shore up our strategies. We can heal. We can do things differently. And we can begin to see ourselves differently.

Because I recognized that God saw me through eyes of patience and compassion, I began seeing myself with compassion. For example, I'd always been categorized as stubborn, as a fighter, but when I saw myself through my life circumstances, I realized that the personality God gave me—that of a passionate fighter— had been good. *It had saved me.*

In my personal journey, I've found some of the hardest parts of stepping out of the tunnel's exit have been knowing myself, identifying who God has created me to be, believing that I am not fully to blame for my unseenness, and being obedient to God despite pushback from others.

I had to find out who I was—who God created me to be— without always jumping straight to *doing.*

"Who are you without doing?" This was the question before me as I stepped out of the tunnel. You'd think I could answer who I am almost immediately, but all the responses that came to mind had some sort of production attached to them.

When I mentally tried to strip away the complex layers of life and remember who I was before I started performing, I remembered once as a young girl creating a circus scene out of folded paper. The idea came to me randomly, and I spent hours in my room, putting reality to my vision. I'm sure it was a sloppy mess, but what I most remember is the joy of creating.

Who am I apart from doing? Here's who: I am sensitive, imaginative, a deep thinker, a fighter, and I have a drive to create. And I am God's, made to enjoy him. *Beauty* has become my key word, drawing me immediately to remember the priority of cultivating presence with God and others. I am always considering ways to cultivate beauty in my surroundings, and in doing so, I feel very "me."

We see ourselves rightly when we look through the lens of Christ's grace and compassion. Because we are never unseen and never unloved, we can come out of hiding and be who we are to the glory of God. God's seeing emboldens us to live lives of worshipful abandon.

What about you, dear reader? What feels very "you"? Perhaps these questions will help you explore what you've hidden even from yourself:

> What do you want that is right and good?
>
> Who were you before others were watching and telling you who you were? If you can remember, who were you before you learned your fig-leaf strategy?

Looking back through the lens of God's grace and compassion, how might you see the wounds and hard parts of your life as opportunities to see God seeing you? How might you have compassion on yourself?

What unique gifts or personality traits do you have that, in enacting, God would receive your worship and, therefore, glory?

Perhaps the most challenging step in responding to God's compassion for those of us who are so used to hiding is stepping out from the self-made shadows and voicing requests, desires, ideas, and needs to those around us.

When I came out of the tunnel, I could no longer stomach some behavior from others I'd accepted and overlooked. I knew I needed to voice my feelings in loving, appropriate ways, which felt frightening and risky, because these were the things that had been dismissed in the past. But I also knew this was part of my growth: letting people know who I really am and advocating for myself in light of Jesus advocating for me.

Additionally, I recognized how hiding my true feelings from others and then growing frustrated with them when they didn't seem to see me was unfair to them. No wonder people felt like they could treat me however they wanted—they didn't know who I was or what I wanted!

In his light, we see others with empathy. In what felt like a huge leap, I disclosed my true feelings regarding my unseenness to those who had hurt me and to those who were close enough to me or to my circumstances to potentially care for me.

As you can probably guess, I received two kinds of responses: those who could not or would not enter into my pain, whether by deflection, blame, apathy, or fear, and those who climbed into the pit with me to help hoist me out.

Those who could not or would not enter compounded my pain, but those who listened, let me cry, and said, "I can see why you feel the way you do," helped my healing.

In other words, what I experienced from those who entered the pit with me was the ministry of presence. Simply offering our tenderhearted presence to a hurting person is a direct reflection of God, who promises multiple times in Scripture that he is with us, will be with us, and will never leave us. His presence to us is perfect peace, comfort, and security and, while we cannot offer perfect presence, we can offer the comfort we ourselves have received from him.[1]

The ministry of presence is marked by empathy. *Empathy* is not total agreement with the perspective of another person but is an agreement that the emotional experience of that person is real.[2] We weep with those who weep from a place of pain.[3]

Sometimes, when we've been sinned against and are fighting to forgive, we need to hear from brothers and sisters, "What happened to you is wrong." Rather than fueling unforgiveness, it clarifies there has actually been a violation, what the violation is, and what specifically we're seeking to forgive.

We will know we're walking well through unseenness when we develop a Spirit-fueled empathy for the overlooked, vulnerable,

---

1. 2 Corinthians 1:4–7.

2. This definition of *empathy* is from a talk given by Andrew Dealy, director of Soul Care and executive director of the Austin Stone Counseling Center.

3. Romans 12:15.

and hurting. We see those people who have been overlooked or dismissed by others. Knowing how that feels, we are quick to seek them out, listen to their stories, pull them into places of connection and service, advocate for them, meet their needs, and remind them of God's love for them.

We "see" others because God first saw us.

Stepping out of the tunnel, I had a newfound and profound depth of empathy I didn't have previously. Those who'd climbed into the pit with me showed me who I want to be and how I want to serve Christ by serving others (often in hidden ways and in hidden moments) rather than serving myself (hoping my service would be seen and validated).

Notice the differing paradigms, one defining my entry into the tunnel and one defining my exit: I walked into the tunnel with self and others as a barometer of the depth of my seenness. I walked out of the tunnel even more committed to serving others, but rather than doing so to gain approval or a sense of security, it is fueled by the desire that others would know their seenness in God. If God asks me to decrease in order that this may happen, I will decrease so that he may increase.

Do you see? *My deepest wounds became my ministry.*

Knowing we're seen by God, we can lay ourselves down in vulnerability, expending less energy on trying to be seen by others and more on seeing and honoring others as God does.

I saw Jesus in those who empathized with me in my own pain, and I thank God for them, but there were those who responded in a different way. Some didn't inquire about the pain I'd disclosed. Some could not hear, accept, and believe it. Some offered platitudes. Some refused to enter into hard conversations.

Though I was angry at these responses in the darkness of the tunnel, I'm not any longer. Rather, God has given me empathy for them. Sometimes it's difficult to face reality. Sometimes what they're hearing or seeing cuts too close to their own unhealed wounds. Sometimes the emotional arena of a person is barricaded and closed off. Sometimes one person's change requires someone they hold close to change as well, and they're not ready for what that will entail. Some people are not ready for the risk of true, intimate relationships where we enter in together without demand or expectation.

That does not make them our enemies. In fact, no man or woman or group of people is our enemy: "For our struggle is not against flesh and blood, but against the rulers, against the authorities, against the cosmic powers of this darkness, against evil, spiritual forces in the heavens" (Eph. 6:12). No one person is an obstacle for our being seen, known, and loved because no one can come between us and God.[4]

And so we can even empathize with those who seem to us like enemies. They may not yet see or understand the truth about God or themselves, an explanation for why they do what they do. By his grace, God has brought us to a place where we can see and understand. Like Jesus on the cross, asking God the Father to forgive those piercing his hands and feet, empathy toward our supposed enemy recognizes that if they could see the truth, they would not be doing what they're doing.[5]

---

4. Romans 8:31–39.

5. Talk given by Andrew Dealy, director of Soul Care and executive director of the Austin Stone Counseling Center at the Austin Stone staff meeting on February 28, 2023.

We know what it's like to walk in darkness or to be blind to what's true, so we can pray for our so-called enemies just as Jesus commanded.

One specific question that has cultivated empathy and, therefore, guided my prayers for those whose responses hurt me is this: How might the person who wounded me have experienced wounds herself? Perhaps considering what you know about those who have wounded you will help you release anger and forgive. Ask God to show you how he sees them.

Empathy for our enemies, however, does not mean we're required to be in close relationships with them. Some people stubbornly refuse to see the truth that's been repeatedly presented to them, and it would be unwise to give our most vulnerable selves to them in relationships. Forgiveness and reconciliation are two different creatures, and we must seek God's wisdom to discern between the two.

At the same time, as I've learned well, it's not our job to convict or set standards of obedience for others. It's not our job to ensure others understand all we've experienced or feel, as if that will heal the wound. It's not our job to make them see us when God already does.

In his light, we see our circumstances from a different angle. If I'm honest, there were many days that I despised the tunnel. To be clear, I despised it every single day until the moment I stepped into the sun on the other side. And then suddenly my heart was overcome with gratitude to God.

Because he awakened me from a dangerous slumber.

He pointed with sorrow at the drifting in our marriage and drove Kyle and me back together, remaking the two of us into something more beautiful than I could have imagined.

He emboldened me to open myself up in vulnerability and need to friends, leading to deeper connections.

He enabled me to forgive.

He heard my cries and delivered me.

He never left me.

He demonstrated to me that I'm not just seen but *wanted*.

And he gave me a ministry.

I wouldn't change my journey through unseenness because it's where I discovered the God Who Sees.

For Further Reflection

1. When we feel "tucked away," how does knowing that our life is hidden in Christ give us profound soul rest?

2. Looking back through the lens of God's grace and compassion, How might you see the wounds and hard parts of your life as opportunities to see God seeing you? How might you have compassion on yourself?

3. What unique gifts or personality traits do you have that, in enacting, God would receive your worship and, therefore, glory?

4. How has walking through unseenness given you compassion for yourself, empathy for others, and given you a fresh perspective on your circumstances?

Conclusion

SEEN THROUGH

G od's deliverance out of my years of unseenness began, as I mentioned previously, with an unexpected word: *wait*.

I wasn't sure what I was waiting for, but I knew *why*. Waiting was a vulnerable response of trust in the Lord's direction, an intentional affront to my lifelong strategies of forward motion through self-agenda, self-sufficiency, and performance—a prolonged act I could only sustain if I believed and lived before the God Who Sees. Waiting, in other words, requires deep courage.

The "old ways," as I began to refer to my long-held rhythms and responses to invisibility and disregard became anathema to me. Similarly, Kyle and I referred to our ingrained marriage patterns in this way, working every day to reject those old ways. In the waiting, God taught us both a new way of living and loving, and I started seeing healthy green sprouts break through the surface where I'd sown my years of sorrow in God. The sprouts almost startled me when they appeared because I'd only sown seeds for so long that I'd begun to doubt a crop of joy would come.

Although the pain was excruciating at times, I'd never experienced such intimacy with God, probably because in no other time of my life had I ever been so aware of my need for him. That intimacy overflowed into intimacy with Kyle and into vulnerability and depth with those friends who'd willingly entered the pit with me.

However, difficult relationships and dynamics remained. Though they were (and are) muddled and confusing, they ironically made my path forward clear: I would no longer accept and absorb some of what I'd long accepted and absorbed.

I felt as if I were wearing ill-fitting clothing—jeans so tight they threatened to cut off my circulation. The jeans were only getting tighter, and my discomfort was only growing. I longed to figuratively rip them off and instead slip on comfortable sweatpants and a lived-in T-shirt. I longed, in other words, to feel fully *me*, not the *me* according to whatever script I could write but rather the *me* God was every day compelling me to be. The trouble was, I simply saw no outlet, no way forward, no ability to affect some of the dynamics I lived in.

And then one day, sitting at my desk, my husband texted me: a friend in Texas had asked him if he'd consider interviewing for a pastoral job. The friend added, "We'd like to talk to Christine about a ministry job as well." Somehow in that moment, I knew that the ground had just shifted beneath our feet.

When I was buried under disregard, when I felt invisible and overlooked, Kyle often asked me, "What is it you want?" He asked not because he was irritated but because he desperately wanted to give it to me. I'd imagined a blurry picture of serving on church staff or working on a team of some sort. I'd envisioned running free without the constant obstacles and brick walls I'd faced.

The opportunity in Texas far exceeded what I'd ever imagined, and it was an opportunity Kyle was eager to take for *me*. For us.

Within a few weeks, the word *wait* became *go* and then it was a subsequent flurry of activity. We said goodbye to people we love, to a church we'd started, and to the home in which we raised our boys. We said hello to new people to love, a new church, and a new home in which to make memories. The griefs and joys combined were often disorienting.

Receiving deliverance, I discovered, requires obedience and courage.

But every day for months after our move, the first words to escape my lips when I opened my eyes were, "Thank you, God." My clothes felt like they fit again.

He had seen me. And when he saw me, rather than standing by idly, he acted. He'd bent down to examine and bind up my wounds. He'd convicted others on my behalf. He'd gently convicted me of my own sin patterns. He'd given me greater intimacy with him and others. He'd enabled me to forgive.

And he'd given me beyond the desires of my heart. I joined our church staff, which by nature of the role, immediately placed me on not one but *two* teams. I watched my husband thrive in his new role. And I am getting to use my gifts in ways I never dreamed could happen.

I have scars. Sometimes something happens that brushes up against those scars, and I feel an electric charge course through my heart. Sometimes I am too aware of being "tucked way," and the fighter in me bucks up—a distrusting, self-protective reaction rooted in the fear of falling back into the pit. Sometimes I remember certain words that were said or specific ways I was treated, and I feel sadness wash over me.

But I simply cannot deny that my God is the God Who Sees. I'm going to hurt and be hurt in this life. I'm not going to see or be seen perfectly by others. But I am safe with him—the faithful One.

I trust him, for he has seen me through.

Remember when we peeked into King David's journal, named the emotions he described in Psalm 142, and observed the pattern of his prayer? At the end of the psalm, we glimpsed David's settled heart as he imagined a future moment when he could tell those gathered around him all the details about how exactly God had delivered him: "Free me from prison so that I can praise your name. The righteous will gather around me because you deal generously with me" (v. 7).

David's psalm has been my guide in writing to you and for you. When I cried to God in my distress and as I journeyed out of the desert with Hagar, I also imagined a future moment when I could tell the glories of God's deliverance. David's vulnerability to share how he emotionally experienced years of disregard and invisibility gave me courage to share my story. Like him, I have not written in hopes of vindication, to blame others, or to establish myself as a victim. I've written to give voice to the experience of unseenness—*your* experience of being overlooked and disregarded. I've written so that you will see and marvel at the God Who Sees you and praise him.

Wherever you find yourself—on the backside of the desert with Hagar, sewing flimsy fig leaves with Eve, plotting your own visibility like Sarai, experiencing Abram's passive apathy, or facing outright attack like David—remember the promised child, the firstborn Son.

Through him, God has "seen to it" that you are forever his.

Because of him I can say with absolute assurance: *You are not forgotten. He will see you through.*

ACKNOWLEDGMENTS

Ashley Gorman at B&H, thank you for your immediate confidence not only in the concept of this book but for being quick to realize how deeply God's been writing this story on my heart and encouraging me to write it for the benefit of others. I've enjoyed working with you on this project.

Andrew Wolgemuth, every time I present an idea to you, you're eager to brainstorm ways to see it come to fruition. Because writers so often work alone, having such partnership, advocacy, and support from you brings me joy and gives me courage.

Susan Hamil, Amy Dodd, Jessica Brumbelow, Jo Franklin, Marylyn Kenney, Tara Bray, and Shannon Blackwell, you were just the friends and confidantes I needed in the wilderness. You would not let me go unseen, and you would not let me stay in the pit, even when it meant climbing in with me and being beside me as long as I needed. Thank you for listening and for helping me make sense of the truth that led me out. I value friendship with each of you so much.

Rich and Sallie Plass at CrossPoint, so much good came out of twenty-four hours with you two. Thank you.

Matt Blackwell and Alison Mezger, I dreamed for years about working on a team, and now I'm on two! Thank you for being a significant part of God's provision and deliverance for me.

To Kyle, who encouraged me to write this book, thank you for leaning in when it would have been easier to lean out. Your tenderness toward me in my pain and your sensitivity toward the Spirit's conviction and leading have marked our wilderness years and have made all the difference for me. I'm thankful for God's precise cut, for, in his wounding, he has given us what we didn't know we needed. I love living in God's deliverance with you!

To the God Who Sees, you saw my need and rescued me. I wake up every day, grateful. I've written these words to praise your name. "I waited patiently for the LORD, and he turned to me and heard my cry for help. He brought me up from a desolate pit, out of the muddy clay, and set my feet on a rock, making my steps secure. He put a new song in my mouth, a hymn of praise to our God. Many will see and fear, and they will trust in the LORD" (Ps. 40:1–3). May it be so.

Appendix A

FEELING WORDS

Angry

Frustrated, critical, annoyed, controlled, mad, bitter, disrespected, furious, jealous, grouchy, irritated

Bad

Guilty, remorseful, confused, criticized, numb, overwhelmed, exhausted, exposed, despised, stressed, pressured, rushed, out of control

Betrayed

Foolish, silly, duped, wounded, let down, humiliated, ridiculed, violated, deceived, misled

Confident

Accepted, trusting, secure, successful, valued, courageous, strong, driven

Disgusted

Disappointed, disapproving, repelled, appalled, revolted, horrified

Happy

Loved, joyful, playful, optimistic, grateful, encouraged, proud, respected, seen, inspired, loving, affectionate

Lonely

Invisible, overlooked, disregarded, ignored, isolated, self-protective, abandoned, rejected, withdrawn, misunderstood, forgotten, excluded

Peaceful

Contented, satisfied, relieved, self-assured

Sad

Despairing, discouraged, weepy, fragile, grieved, depressed, hurt, ashamed, vulnerable, empty, crushed, desperate, hopeless

Scared

Fearful, anxious, unsettled, frightened, unsafe, uneasy, nervous, hypervigilant, cautious, indecisive, hesitant, guarded, distressed, burdened, threatened, inadequate

Surprised

Shocked, excited, astonished, disillusioned, awestruck, stunned, disturbed

Appendix B

ATTRIBUTES OF GOD[1]

Attentive // God hears and responds to the needs of his children.

Compassionate // God cares for his children and acts on their behalf.

Creator // God made everything. He is uncreated.*[2]

Deliverer // God rescues and saves his children.

Eternal // God is not limited by and exists outside of time.

Faithful // God always keeps his promises.

Generous // God gives what is best and beyond what is deserved.

Glorious // God displays his greatness and worth.*

---

1. Taken from *Psalms: The Prayers of God's People* by The Village Church.

2. Starred definitions are taken from or informed by *The ABCs of God* by Children Desiring God.

Good // God is what is best and gives what is best. He is incapable of doing harm.

Holy // God is perfect, pure, and without sin.*

Incomprehensible // God is beyond our understanding. We can comprehend him in part but not in whole.

Infinite // God has no limits in his person or on his power.

Immutable/Unchanging // God never changes. He is the same yesterday, today, and tomorrow.

Jealous // God will not share his glory with another. All glory rightfully belongs to him.

Just // God is fair in all his actions and judgments. He cannot overpunish or underpunish.

Loving // God feels and displays infinite unconditional affection toward his children. His love for them does not depend on their worth, response, or merit.

Merciful // God does not give his children the punishment they deserve.

Omnipotent/Almighty // God holds all power. Nothing is too hard for God. What he wills he can accomplish.

Omnipresent // God is fully present everywhere.

Omniscient // God knows everything: past, present, and future; all potential and real outcomes; all things micro and macro.

Patient/Long-Suffering // God is untiring and bears with his children.

Provider // God meets the needs of his children.

Refuge // God is a place of safety and protection for his children.*

Righteous // God is always good and right.

Self-Existent // God depends on nothing and no one to give him life or existence because he has life within himself.

Self-Sufficient // God is not vulnerable. He has no needs.

Sovereign // God does everything according to his plan and pleasure. He controls all things.

Transcendent // God is not like humans. He is infinitely higher in being and action.

Truthful // Whatever God speaks or does is truth and reality.

Wrathful // God hates all unrighteousness.

Wise // God knows what is best and acts accordingly. He cannot choose wrongly.

Worthy // God deserves all glory and honor and praise.